A Breath of Fresh Air

GarlicPress

# Substitute Ingredients

## S. Harold Collins

### Lorraine Wilde-Oswalt

Published by:
Garlic Press
100 Hillview Lane #2
Eugene, OR 97401

ISBN 0-931993-01-6
Reorder Number GP-001

# TABLE OF INGREDIENTS

# PREFACE

This is the second edition of **Substitute Ingredients.** The text has been only slightly revised and simple cosmetic arrangements have been included to lend the book a higher polish. Otherwise, this is the same **Substitute Ingredients** that we offered in 1974.

The cookbook format of **Substitute Ingredients** has proven popular while emphasizing the separate offerings of Langauage Arts, Mathematics, and Art. The Master Sheets which complement most lessons are easily reproducible. And we hope you will share our sense of humor, a quality we hold so important to any teaching role.

SHC
Garlic Press
1989

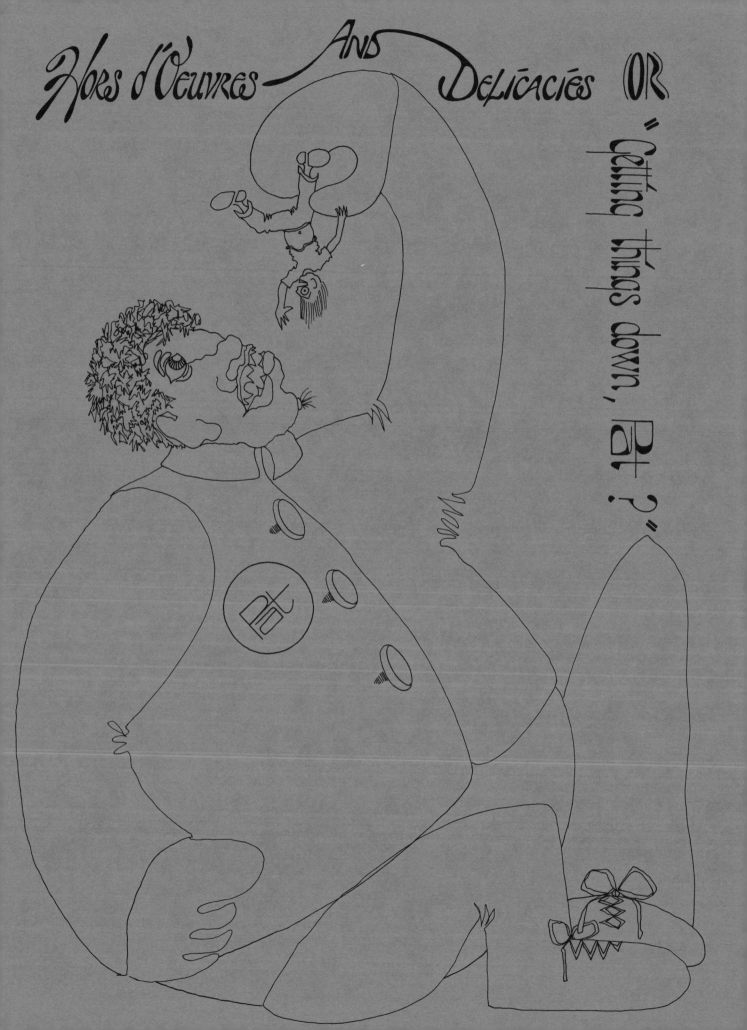

# Hors d'Oeuvres and Delicacies

### For the Substitute Teacher

I have been a Substitute Teacher most of my credentialed life, the exception being a short stint as a regular Classroom Teacher. And one thing a Substitute Teacher learns quickly is that those professionals for whom they are replacements are often very casual (sometimes spelled *careless*) about lesson plans and assignments. In an effort to remedy awkward situations and to ease the progress of a normal school day, I have come to depend upon my *bag of goodies* -a briefcase loaded with a variety of lessons and activities. Thus when lesson plans are not present, or when a large amount of time is allotted to an unreasonable activity ("From 8:30 - 10:00, have students read to themselves."), or when the composure of a class is noticeably upset by the absence of the regular Classroom Teacher, or when any number of other variables exists, I disappear behind my briefcase, dig, rummage, and find a lesson that will best suit the classroom situation.

I feel that when a Substitute Teacher becomes responsible to create and present his or her own lessons and activities, he or she has become professionally credible. And in a job role that all too often casts the Substitute Teacher as a mere babysitter, the credible Substitute is aiding to perfect the reputation of Substitute Teachers generally while maintaining quality education.

Because a Substitute Teacher remains for only a short time in a specific classroom, the lessons and activities that can be presented must be short and direct. But most important, they must be engaging. There are numerous publications that compile games and activities for short span lessons. Unfortunately, most of these lack either interest or merit. Realizing this, I have developed, for my bag of goodies, a wide variety of lessons and activities that, when accompanied by simple preparation, produce engaging, enjoyable, and valuable results.

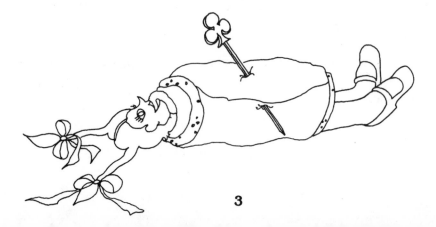

3

For the Classroom Teacher

If you have read the preceding section, I hope you will appreciate my concern for Substitute Teachers. Substitute Teachers have a very hard position to fill, especially if they resent the stereotypical role of babysitter. I am sure you would like your classroom conducted, in your absence, by a person capable of surpassing the babysitting bounds. Hopefully this publication will enable that person who temporarily conducts your class to conduct a day of education that is meaningful and productive for your students.

Don't think this publication is solely for the Substitute Teacher! It has proper use for you, the Classroom Teacher. Keeping in mind that these lessons are intended for short presentations and direct results, you can easily extend them to fill the time and needs of your normal teaching goals. Then again there are those gaps that occur in classroom teaching when short presentations and direct results are satisfactory. However you choose to use this publication, you will find its contents suitable ingredients for teaching.

How to Use This Here Thing

I have directed my lessons to cover third through eighth grades. Yes, that is a very wide span of ages and abilities, but most of these lessons, in one form or another, are applicable to those grade levels. As long as you recognize that adjustments are necessary to compensate for grade and ability level, these lessons will prove highly practical.

There are four courses to this menu: Art, Math, Language Arts, and Humor. Each section contains a varying number of lessons, with subject matter often overlapping. But usually each lesson provides a lead-in, practical comments, and a resulting activity. In addition, most lessons have **Master Sheets** suitable for reproduction.

When possible appropriate lessons are followed with references to supplementary materials.

This publication contains all the necessary ingredients for successful and fresh classroom learning, whether you are a Substitute Teacher or a regular Classroom Teacher.

# Mandalas

Coloring has very subtle values that are all too often dismissed. This is due in part to the traditional coloring books that require little more of a child than to fill in common shapes and figures, forsaking creativity and imagination. Yet, kids have unappeaseable appetites for coloring. They will absorb themselves in it for prolonged periods with the most devout attention.

Mandala coloring offers a number of creative values, allowing a child to express certain inner qualities through abstractions of color, shape, grouping, and line. Psychologists have long realized that colors and configurations accurately reflect inner emotions, feelings, moods, and preceptions. Mandala coloring allows many of these inner qualities a means of expression.

Mandalas do not require the participant to arrive at the preconceived shapes and themes so common to traditional coloring. Stop for a minute. Take a long look at one of the following mandalas. Don't your eyes begin to emphasize certain groupings? Aren't you able mentally to color the shapes and lines that you emphasize? The involvement in patterns and colors becomes very intense as particiaption increases. Try coloring one of the mandalas yourself !

Once a mandala has been completed in all its splendor of color and shape, cut it out and mount it on a piece of colored construction paper. The construction paper will lend a striking background.

# A Joy at any Price ✳

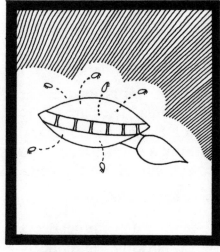

**what is this ?**

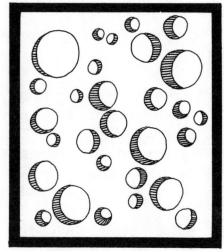

**What is this ?**

Did you recognize the first one as a *Fleaing UFO* ? and the second one as *The Cover to the Holy Bible* ? (No hissing, please!)

You may remember a rather bespeckled cartoonist named Roger Price. Roger is responsible for *Droodles*, which was a daily syndicated cartoon appearing in many newspapers. Roger's strange creations were always supplemented by outrageous explanations.

Roger's Droodles were never intended to be highly refined cartoons, but instead simple scrawlings that allowed one's imagination to provide a suitable title.

Roger has published two selected collections of Droodles. Not only is his Droodles humor priceless, but their classroom application provides a spark for a creativity and imagination.

For a class lesson, I have taken several Droodles and drawn then on large pieces of posterboard. During different periods of the day, as an icebreaker in the morning, as a settling factor after recess, or as an enlivenment in the afternoon, I place several Droodles before the class for scrutiny.

I usually present the initial Droodle in this manner: "I want to show you a few masterpieces of art that you will recognize immediately. You've all seen them before and there will be little need of my telling you much about them.  Take this one for instance ... "

Of course you have set them up to expect a classic work, and when they see the first Droodle they are taken aback.  They will quickly respond to the intended humor and you will be able to call for possible explanations of individual Droodles.

After you have heard a number of possible explantions, explain what it really is.

By the end of the day (the Classroom Teacher can present this lesson over a longer time) the kids are fully acquainted with Droodles.  They are ready to create their own.  There is a Droodle Master Sheet that can be reproduced on art paper.  The Master Sheet is simply a square form into which the student can draw their own creations.  You can also encourage the students to place a title below the square.

Here are some practical comments as to what the kids will produce: don't expect subtle wit or sophisticated humor in their creations.  Some kids will do no more than draw what seems a regular picture.  This is fine in itself.  Children develop sophisticated humor very slowly,  for humor is a very special concept that even adults grasp only after lengthy exposure to its great variety.

What kids will produce as a Droodle may seem to an adult a clumsy or a humorless picture.  But there is always some connection between the picture and the student's thoughts.

For some kids the actual creation of a single Droodle will take only a few minutes, so encourage them to do more than one Droodle.  The ideas for the four Droodles drawn into this lesson-discussion are student creations.  If you enjoy them as much as I do, then you'll understand why I feel Droodles are A JOY AT ANY PRICE.

*Droodles #1.  Droodles #2.*  Roger Price; Price, Stern, Sloan Publishers, Los Angeles, California.

Title :

Looking up a nose.

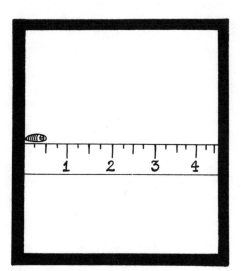

Yup! A half grown inch worm!

Let me make this very plane; making paper airplanes requires a great deal of teacher coordination and a great deal of student self-control. If these respective elements are missing, this exercise will end as an aerial disaster. It is fun for kids to make paper airplanes and even more fun to fly them and fly them. If you, as a teacher, are unable to impress the necessity for self-control, thirty kids each flying their newly made paper airplane will become a frantic spectacle.

Don't be dissuaded from this lesson; just gain the cooperation of the students.

## PATTERNS AND INSTRUCTIONS

All four paper airplanes are designed to be made on 8 1/2 by 11 inch paper; the heavier the the better. Instructions are often difficult for kids to follow, so instructions for these airplanes are a combination of illustrations and writing.

Hint: All paper airplanes have outside borders which are defined as rectangles slightly smaller than the length and width of the page. Kids will need to cut to the outside border before beginning to fold or decorate the individual planes. Throughout the lesson, emphasize repeatedly that clowning and disruptive action will not be appreciated.

Allow the kids some time to go outside for practical flight-testing. Stage a few contests: for distance, for time aloft, and for aerobatics.

I would suggest that you construct sample models prior to class time. This will aid you in helping the kids; for some children surely have construction problems.

# Distance Model #1 — directions

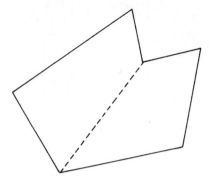

① fold on center line and then lay flat again.

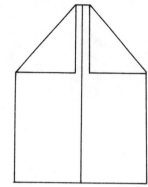

② fold the corners in on lines marked with a Ⓖ

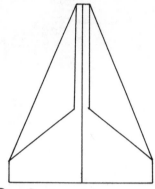

③ fold again on lines marked with an Ⓡ

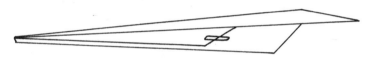

This is a fine distance plane! Be sure to make it out of good quality paper and tape it as in step ⑥ then give it a good strong throw at a slight upward angle and watch it as it flies straight and true like an arrow.

⑤ fold the wings down on lines marked with a Ⓩ

⑥ Tape across the top of the plane and also underneath to keep it as sleek and wind resistant as possible.

④ fold backwards on the center line

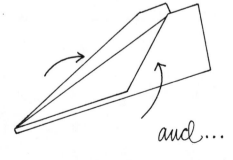

and...

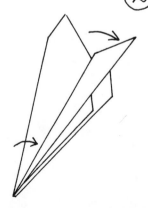

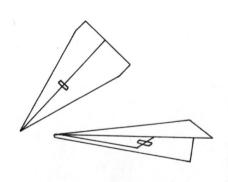

Distance ~ "Model #1

G    G
R    R
N  N

# Time Aloft ~ model #2 directions

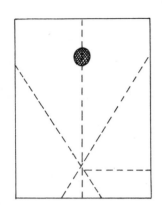

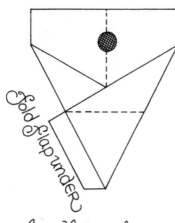
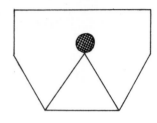

Cut out finger hole fold along dotted lines ......

Fold flap under

To this shape. Turn the plane OVER ....

then fold the tip of the plane to the REAR

* This plane is really great for Loop-t-Loops. Be sure to use finger hole when launching.

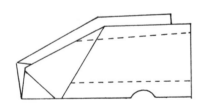

Now, fold the plane along the center line . . . .

next ⟶

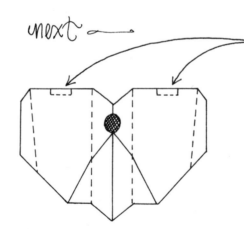

Fold wings & wing tips down on dotted lines as in this top view

and finally cut the flaps and try them in different positions when testing your plane. You'll find one position for them that really makes your plane fly at its best.

Now color the designed areas of your plane and take flight !

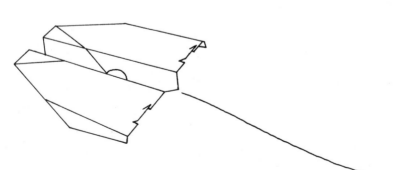

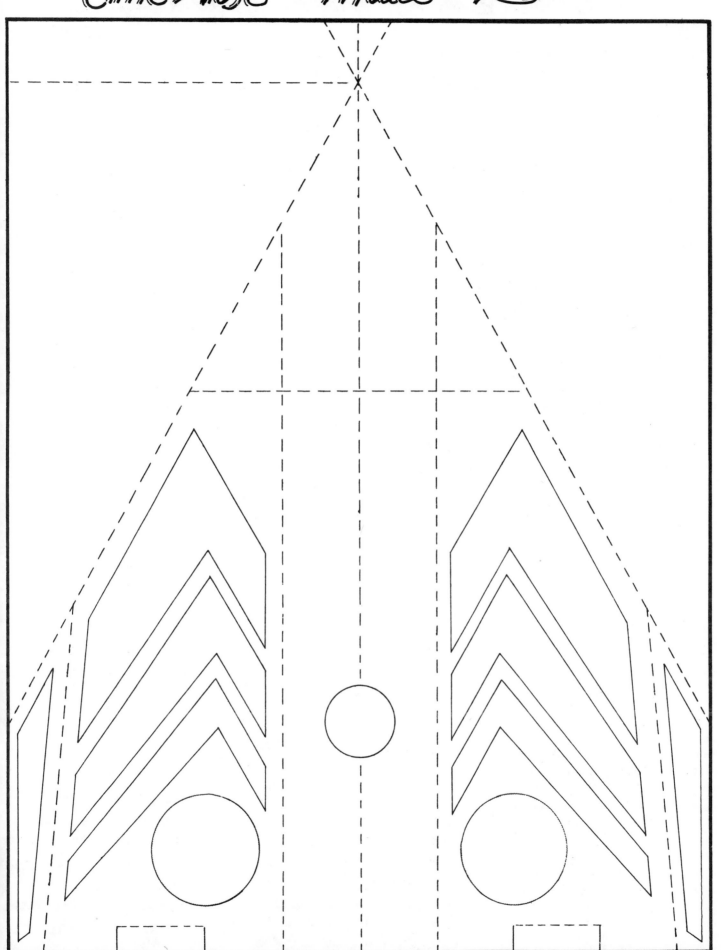

Time Aloft ~ Model # 2

# Aero-Bird – Model #3 directions

Tail Section

Cut off tail section.
Crease paper on
dotted lines.
①

Refold paper to
this shape.
②

Fold points
Down toward the
Pointed front of the
plane.
③

Crease and unfold on
these 3 dotted lines.
④

This is a really fine little plane — it should be launched gently and remember to play around with the tail tips for flight variety.

You'll notice that this plane looks like a bird in flight and how it seems to defy gravity and dares to stay in the air, lifting about like a real bird ♥

⑦ Turn the plane over ...

(top view →)

⑥

fold

⑤

fold in the sides as shown
below and then push
them together as arrows
indicate.

Insert the tail section as
shown, pointed end, first &
make sure the pointed
end goes all the way into
the cone of the plane.
Then fold the lower section
back, leaving point out front.

and fold the wings &
tail section toward
you on the center line.
Then fold the tail tips
up toward you and
experiment with them
in different positions.

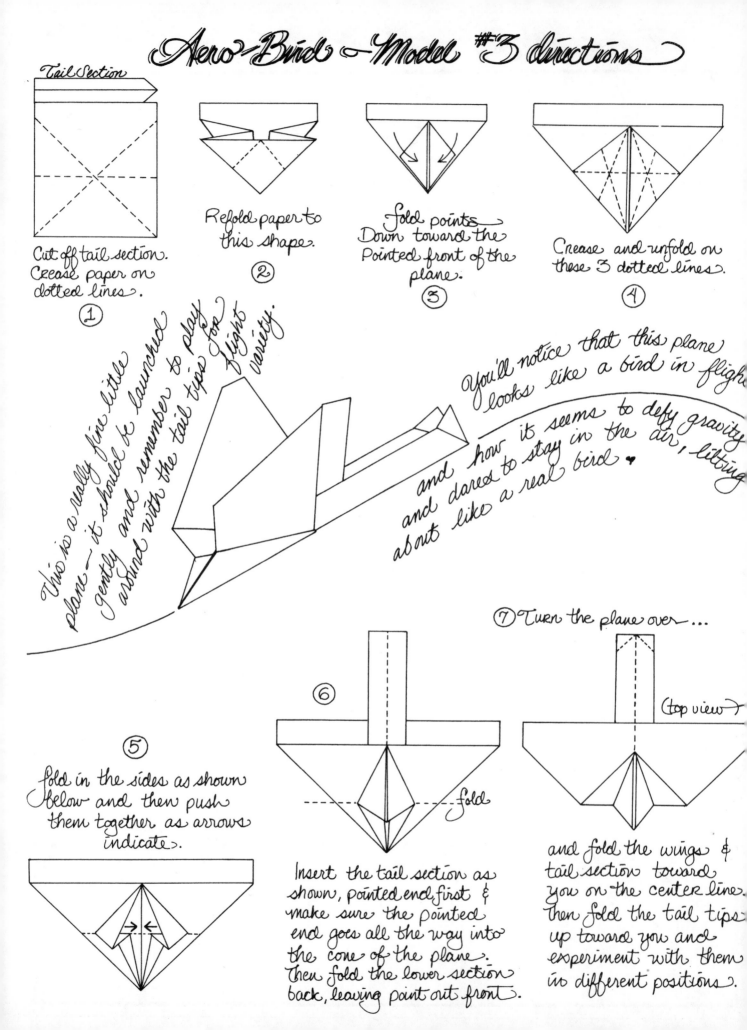

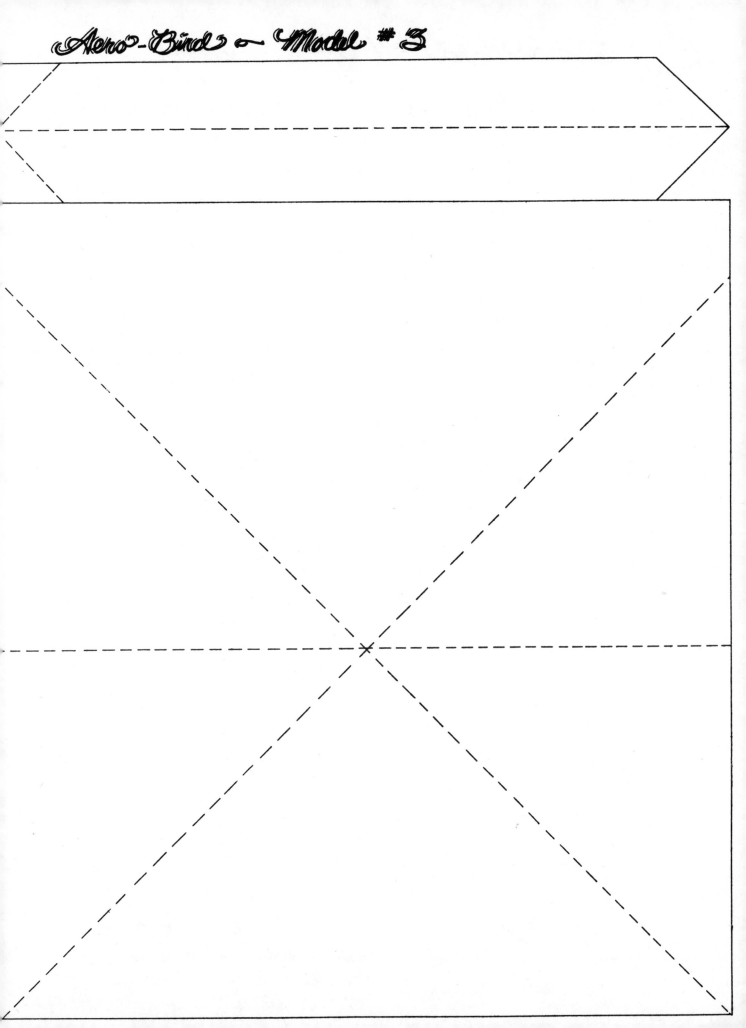

Aero-Bird ~ Model # 3

# Duration Model #4 ~ directions

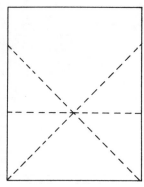

① Make three folds on these dotted lines

② and then

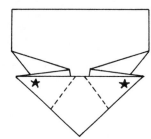

Fold in the sides as shown above.

③ fold corner points (★)

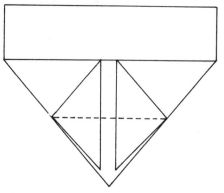

down, leaving about a ¼" space down the middle.

This can be a nice plane but you have to be willing to experiment around a bit. It wants to be a good plane, but it really nice roll back and flies upside

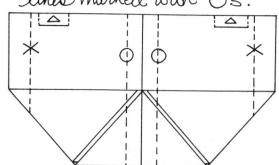

Sometimes it does a down for you. needs your help.

patient with it and

④ fold the tip of the plane up on

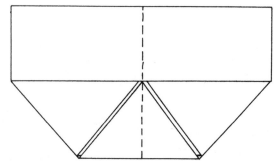

the dotted line shown in ③ and then fold up on the center dotted line shown here.

⑤ Fold wings down on the dotted lines marked with ○'s.

and fold the wing tips up on the dotted lines marked with ✕'s. Cut and fold up the wing flaps (△'s)

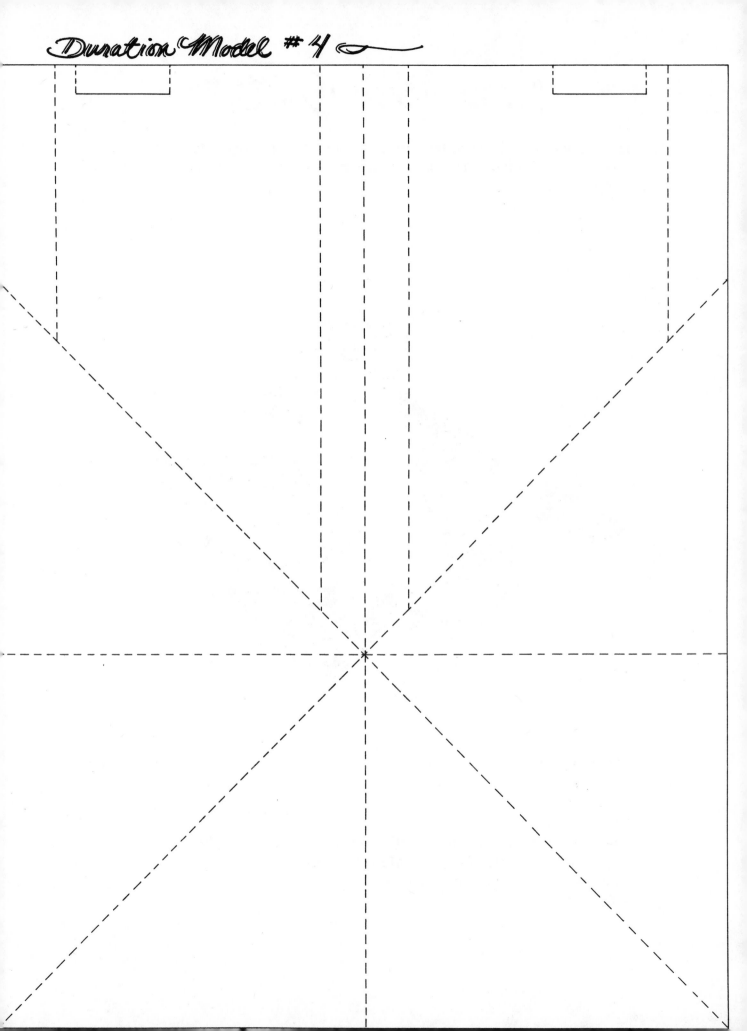

Duration Model # 4

# The Art in Tan

This very simple lesson, best presented to grades three, four, or five, is an offshoot of the tangram lesson presented in the Math Section (refer to *Tangrams* ).

## MATERIALS AND EQUIPMENT

Scissors .
Paste
Two colored tangram squares (the 3-inch squares supplied as Master
    Sheets for the Tangram Math lesson)
One sheet of drawing or construction paper.

## WHAT IS DONE

1. Cut out the seven tangram pieces for each 3-inch square (14 parts total).
2. Create a design, story, or figure using all or part of the 14 tangram pieces.
3. When the design, story, figure, toy, animal, etc., has been fully created pasted or glue the result onto drawing or construction paper, recreating the desired subject.

# Geometricks

Here are three geometric shapes that can be assembled as individual projects or assembled for a mobile. All shapes invite the accent lent by crayons, or felt pens, or colored pencils. Each shape provides a small illustration to give the kids an idea of the assembled shapes.

Assembling the shapes will give rise to possible confusion. Kids will often mismatch corners that are to be glued. Stress that corners, when glued, must form a complete shape and that their powers of observation will help match the correct illustrations, and consequently construct the desired shape. For instance, take the octahedron (please!), it is very complex in its plane surfaces as well as its illustrations, but most kids, if given the time, can properly complete the shape by matching the illustrations while referring to the small assembled drawing provided on the Master Sheets.

**The Tetrahedron.** As with the other two Geometricks, this shape is a progression of events. When asembled the tetrahedron shows a dog chasing a cat, which is chasing a mouse, which is after a hunk of cheese.

**The Triangular Dipyramid.** The progression on this shape is the evolution of a clown's face, by stages. Beginning with just an oval face and a round nose, the clown evolves through five further stages before it fully flourishes. Encourage the kids to add their own face compositions to the first two incomplete faces.

**The Octahedron.** This Esher-esque creature is a baby alligator emerging from an egg. The most complicated shape and illustration, it will need greater care in assembling.

# A Geometricks Create-A-Shape #1

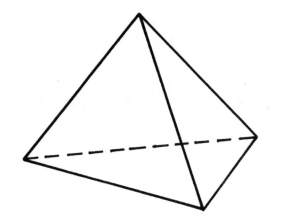

You will be making a

# TETRAHEDRON

ⓐ Cut just inside
the dashing line,
all around the
border.

ⓑ then —
fold on all
other lines
and...

ⓒ match the cheese,
the cat, and the dog
and glue!

# A Geometricks Create-A-Shape #2

You will be making a

## TRIANGULAR DIPYRAMID

(a.) Cut just inside the dashing line, all around the border.

(b.) then fold on all other lines, match the clowns, and glue!

# A Geometricks Create-A-Shape #3

You will be making an

# OCTAHEDRON

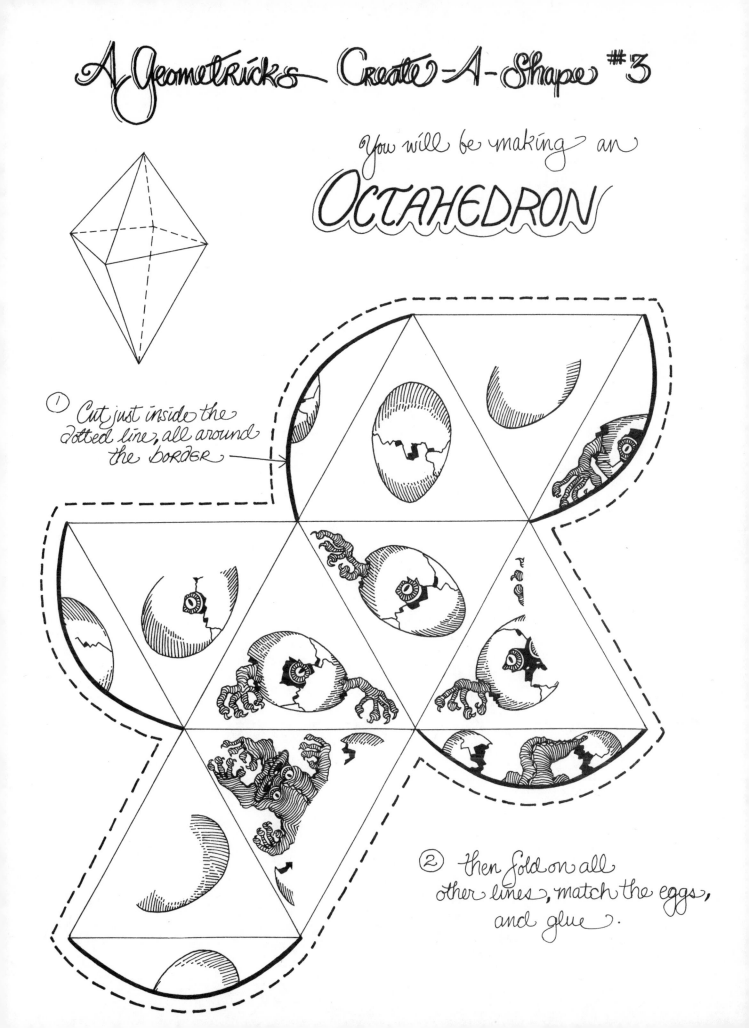

① Cut just inside the dotted line, all around the border

② then fold on all other lines, match the eggs, and glue.

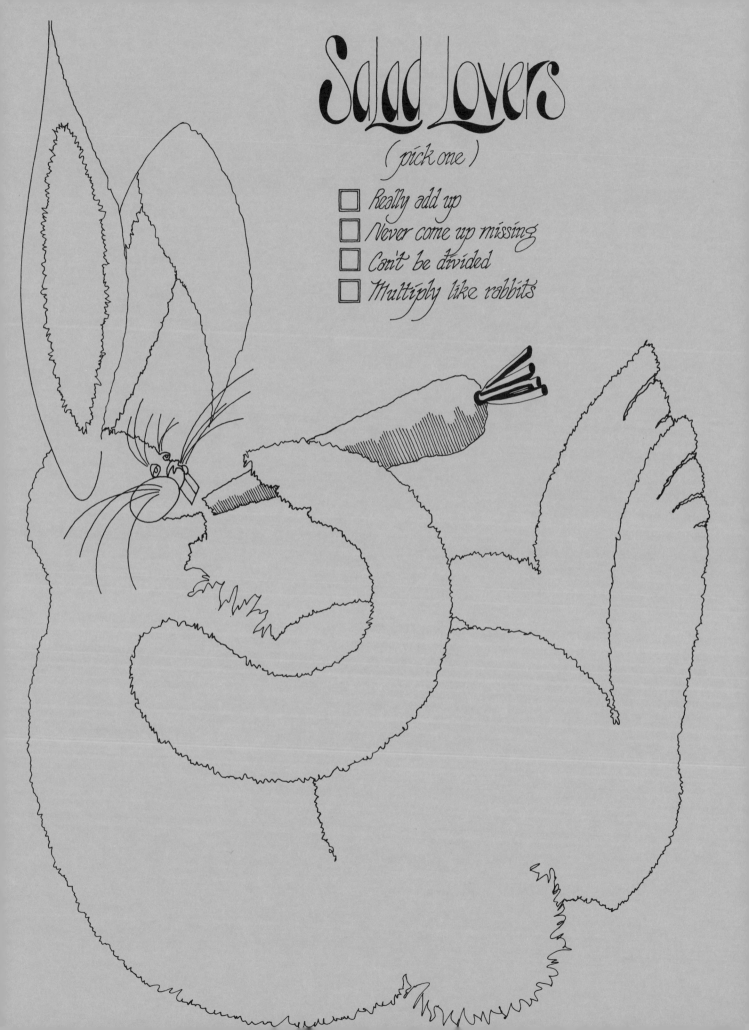

# Salad Lovers

## (pick one)

- ☐ *Really add up*
- ☐ *Never come up missing*
- ☐ *Can't be divided*
- ☐ *Multiply like rabbits*

# "I've been inducted into Math" or "Be Reasonable"

There was an old Steve Allen comic routine called *The Answer Man*. The Answer Man would provide answers to questions before the questions were ever asked. The routine reversed the normal question-answer sequence common to deductive thinking. Playing off of The Answer Man, here is a math lesson that gives answers and requires the kids to provide the sequence that will explain the given answers. It is largely an inductive process applied to math.

The lesson provides, in problem 12, a means for correcting the answers for problems one through eleven. Other than a few distractions in several problems, the lesson is intented to make the kids reason backwards to determine what combination of purchases provides a given answer.

Direct the kids' attention to the sign, with its prices, and particularly the LIMIT OF 4 EACH. They can not buy more than four of any one item. Sometimes, you will need to explain the contextual meaning of *least* (problem 1) and *greater* (problem 2). Without further direction, the kids are ready to begin problems 1 through 11. Indicate they do not need to do the last problem at this time.

After sufficient time has elapsed to complete the problems, direct everyone's attention to the last question. This is a schedule of purchases in combination, cars to candy bars. It is their key to correcting the preceeding problems.

Illustrate on the board how they are to go about completing the schedule (the first five prices have been provided). Along the top are possible candy purchases, along the side are possible toy car purchases.

> No toy cars, one candy bar purchase = 3¢
> No toy cars, two candy bar purchases = 6¢
> No toy cars, three candy bar purchases = 9¢  etc.
>
> One toy car, no candy bar purchase = 5¢
> One toy car, one candy bar purchase = 8¢
> One toy car, two candy bar purchases = 11¢  etc.

Allow time for the kids to complete the schedule.

The numbers that are filled in can be used to correct problems 1 through 11. For instance, problem 3:

> A girl spent 8¢, what did she buy?
> (1.) Find 8¢ on the schedule (there is only one).
> (2.) Read up to the number of candy bars.
> (3.) Read across to the number of toy cars.
>      Answer: One car, one candy bar.

Problems 4, 5, and 11 have distractions. They require some means to determine the money spent before the types of purchases can be computed.

Correct the problems by using the schedule and make any explanations necessary. The kids can keep their own papers for corrections.

Smitty's ✪ Toys Etc.
Small Toy Cars    5¢ each
Candy Bars        3¢ each
· limit of 4 each ~·.

NAME_____

1.  What is the least amount of money you can spend?
2.  What is the greatest?
3.  A girl spent 8¢, what did she buy?
4.  Helen gave the clerk a dime and a nickel, she received 2¢ change. What did she buy?
5.  Fred borrowed 2¢ and added it to his 30¢ allowance. If he spent it all, what did he buy?
6.  Eggbert spent 17¢. What did he buy?
7.  Could anyone spend exactly 25¢? How?
8.  What purchases amount to 21¢?
9.  How many different purchases could be made if you had enough money?
10. How many ways could you spend 18¢?
11. Weird Wanda had four pennies. She exchanged them with Barb Wire for a nickel. She exchanged her nickel with Sally Mander for a dime. She exchanged the dime for two nickels and five pennies with Perry Chute. She pays Barb back her penny and Sally back her nickel. On the way to the store, she found a quarter. If she saves 23¢ what can she buy with the rest of her money?
12. Complete the following schedule:

What's This?

(Backwards: Hot Rod)

CANDY BARS 3¢

|   |   | 0 | 1 | 2 | 3 | 4 | 5 |
|---|---|---|---|---|---|---|---|
| T | 0 | 0 | 3 | 6 | 9 |   |   |
| O | 1 | 5 |   |   |   |   |   |
| Y |   |   |   |   |   |   |   |
| C | 2 | 10 |   |   |   |   |   |
| A | 3 |   |   |   |   |   |   |
| R | 4 |   |   |   |   |   |   |
| S 5¢ | 5 |   |   |   |   |   |   |

# Geometry of Squares

An absorbing lesson that can lead to many others centers around a pair of three-inch squares.

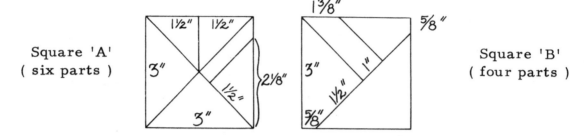

Square 'A'
( six parts )

Square 'B'
( four parts )

**MATERIALS: Squares, Parts, and Envelopes.**

To present a class lesson you will need:
   (1.) 30 three-inch squares (15 for **A** type squares and 15 for **B** type squares).
   (2.) 30 envelopes.

Made from heavy cardboard (or tagboard or posterboard) these squares should be cut into their respective parts and placed in individual envelopes. All A squares will have six parts, and all B squares will have four parts.

## LABELING

Labeling is very important, otherwise parts and envelopes will be easily scattered, mixed, or lost. First, color label the envelopes. For instance, in blue felt pen, mark all A envelopes as: **A (six parts)**. With a red felt pen, mark all B envelopes as: **B (four parts)**.

Second, and most important, because there are a number of A and B squares in simultaneous use, you must have a method that will allow you to identify to which square each individual part belongs. Such a method allows you to return stray parts to appropariate squares, and also reduces any confusion among students who mix parts.

Here is a method I use: I carry 30 envelopes (you can make more or less depending upon your need), 15 labeled A and 15 labeled B. I have assigned each of these a number between 1 and 30. I have chosen to label all A squares with a number between 1 and 15, and all B squares with a number between 16 and 30. I have written the assigned number on the back of each piece composing a particular square. For instance, I have assigned one of the A squares the number 10. This indicates that I have labeled all six pieces of that square (and that square only) with a 10 on the backside of each piece.

If a loose part is found with a 10 on the back, I simply ask, "Who has an A envelope with a 10 on the back of each piece?" And the part is returned. An identification such as this also works well to solve any other problems concerning scattered parts.

## DIRECTIONS AND PROCEDURES.

Instructions are imperative before the envelopes are distribluted. Instructions should establish the necessity of : (1.) not losing parts, and (2.) not exchanging envelope contents. It's remarkable that despite the many times I have used this lesson, I have rarely lost a part, even when 30 envelopes are used; that is 150 separate parts.

Explain that you have two kinds of envelopes. "One is marked with an A and contains 6 parts; the other is marked with a B and contains 4 parts. Everyone will have a chance to work with both, so you need not feel that the person next to you will be doing something you won't be doing.

"In a moment I'm going to give each of you an envelope. You are responsible for checking to see if your envelope has 6 parts if it's an A square, or 4 parts if it's a B square. Don't exchange parts to preform this exercise."

Hold up an uncut three-inch square as a model.

"Whether you have an A square or a B square, you have the correct number of parts to make a square this size."

Pass out the envelopes, alternating between A and B. As soon as the kids have received their envelopes, they can begin constructing their three-inch square.

Circulate, possibly saying: "Don't think you can make a square lickety-split. It takes awhile to maneuver those parts around."

You might take, as an aid, your three-inch square and say that you are willing to trace around it (on a piece of paper) for anyone who wants the square form as a guide. Many will.

Allow time for investigation. If kids become frustrated, give a hint for each square; you can draw the hints on the blackboard or you can draw them for each student individually on a piece of his or her own paper.

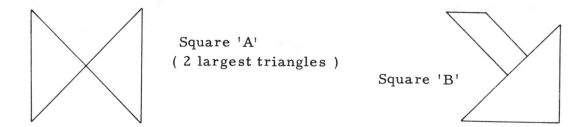

Square 'A'
( 2 largest triangles )

Square 'B'

Some kids will assemble their squares faster than others. Have those who finish quickly experiment with their parts to make other geometric shapes. This is particularly good for the A squares. Here are other shapes that can be made with the six part of the A square:

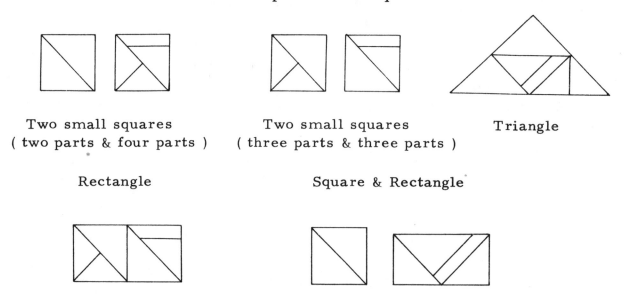

Two small squares
( two parts & four parts )

Two small squares
( three parts & three parts )

Triangle

Rectangle

Square & Rectangle

Challenge an A assembler, who has finished quickly, to make:

(1.) 2 small squares with two parts in one square and 4 parts in the other, or
(2.) 2 small squares with 3 parts in one square and 3 parts in the other, or
(3.) a rectangle using all of the parts, or
(4.) a square and a rectangle using all of the parts, or
(5.) a triangle using all of the parts.

Square B is the least versatile. Early finishers can be encouraged to experiment with their parts to make other geometric shapes, too.

After enough time, tell everyone to stop. "If you have an A square, count the six parts. Put them into the envelope. If you have a B square, count the four parts. Put them into the envelope.

"Exchange with someone who has the opposite lettered envelope and construct the new square."

Circulate again, giving help and encouragement. Allow time for all to finish or experiment fully. At this juncture, you have a number of alternatives:

(1.) end the lesson, having all parts counted and returned to their respective envelopes;
(2.) collect all parts and envelopes, and pass out an uncut three-inch square for each student to make his or her own square-puzzle;
(3.) encourage the kids to make geometric shapes with the parts of their A or B square.

This is a way to get them to make creations -geometric or fantasy (sailboats, houses, butterfiles, faces, trees). But have them record their creations on paper. Recording means illustrating how the parts (they don't have to use them all) combine to make a created shape.

Note: This lesson is really fantastic. Don't be skeptical because there are so many parts or envelopes. All that is required to coordinate the lesson are <u>clear</u> and <u>repeated</u> verbal instructions. Kids become very engrossed. It does take preparation as far as assembling the three-inch squares, cutting them, and labeling them as will as the envelopes; but it is well worth it. I am sure you will find more variations than those mentioned above.

# Pick a Number (1)

Ask the kids to take out a piece of scratch paper, any old piece; it will be for their use only. Tell them to pick a number between 1 and 10 and to write it on their paper. Tell them you don't want to know what the number is.

So that you can talk about their number, you are going to assign it a letter value, let's say Z. Write Z on the board. Observe that there can be 10 different Z's in the room, one for every number from 1 to 10. Someone, no doubt, has chosen 5, someone has chosen 9, and someone else has probably chosen 3. But so you can talk about everyone's number, you're letting Z stand for everyone's number.

To their Z, have them add 9 (hint: always start with addition and make the number large). Show that it is merely a simple addition problem. As a result of adding 9 to their Z, they have a sum. Next, from their sum, whatever it is, subtract, let's say, 5. They will now have a new answer.

$$
\begin{array}{r}
Z \\
+\ 9 \\
-\ 5 \\
+\ 7 \\
-\ 8 \\
+\ 4 \\
\end{array}
$$

Continue with addition or subtraction combinations for three or four more numbers. For instance: add 7, subtract 8, and add 4.

You should be writing the individual steps, as they occur, on the board. Those steps would look like the example to the right.

$$
\begin{array}{r}
9 \\
-\ 5 \\
\hline
4 \\
+\ 7 \\
\hline
11 \\
-\ 8 \\
\hline
3 \\
+\ 4 \\
\hline
7 \\
\end{array}
$$

## LAST STEP

Have them subtract the original number that they chose, their Z. Wait a sufficient time, and then ask, by a show of hands, how many have come up with 7?

General Amazement (you know him, he's a friend of Major Blunder) will prevail. The kids will want to know how you did it!

40

<u>The Secret</u>, if you haven't figured it out: you merely add and subtract the numbers between the Z's. The number they pick, Z, is in effect cancelled out at the end  when you ask for its subtraction in the last step.

At this point, I tell the kids, "I don't read minds or have ESP, or perform magic.  I'm merely doing a trick.  Let's do it again.  And this time be on your toes to discover my trick.  You might want to take it home and play it on a brother, a sister, a parent, or a friend."

Again ask them to pick a number, any number they want.  Suggest that they keep their number small, since smaller numbers are easier to work with.

But this time instead of telling them the numbers to add and subtract, say you will take numbers from them, if they'll raise their hands -they'll be eager to participate.

Assign, again, a letter value to their chosen number.  And be sure to start with a positive number.  You might point out that they don't have to follow a + - + - order when they suggest numbers.

After the second time through, ask for speculation as to what you are doing so that you and each student are ending the same number.

You can repeat the exercise several times, depending on the attentiveness of the group.  You'll probably have to draw the answer out of them:
      (1.) All you are doing is adding and subtracting the suggested numbers;
      (2.) And the chosen number they start with is cancelled out by the last step, subtracting it.  Therefore their picking of an original number is a diversion.

I add a little drama to the act.  Just before I tell them to subtract the original number (the last step), I write the answer rather secretively on the board, but cover it simultaneously with my free hand.  This way they match their answer to mine.  They are assured I'm not just making it up and that I'm not looking on someone's paper.

This exercise can take anywhere from 10 to 20 minutes, depending upon the interest of the kids and your presentation.

The tangram has become a very popular device for mathematical explorations. Originating in China, the tangram was first introduced in the Western world among nobles and aristocrats. And since its introduction in the United States during the early nineteenth century, it has enjoyed several periods of popularity. In recent years it has been an important device for stressing concepts in new math.

Tangrams provide countless math exercises. Here is only one, again directed at a quick presentation, followed by a practical exercise. The lesson includes three Master Sheets: two Master Sheets comprise the exercises that the kids will do; and a third Master Sheets contains the tangrams needed for the exercises (the tangram squares are also used for *The Art In Tan* ; see the Art section). When you reproduce the tangram Master Sheet, the best reproduction is on heavy construction paper, tagboard, or cardboard.

## INSTRUCTIONS AND PROCEDURES

Ask if the kids have their own scissors. If not, you had better determine where a number can be found. Not every student will need scissors, so sharing will be appreciated. Prepare the kids with a brief explanation of the origin of this seven-part square. Pass out the square, indicating that they have to cut out the seven pieces that compose their tangram square. Be sure to emphasize that the excess paper from cutting should be put in the nearest wastebasket.

Once the parts have been cut out, have the kids practice reassembling the seven parts into the three inch square. Reassembly will provide further acquaintence with the seven parts.

After a few minutes, regain everyone's attention. Tell the kids that they will get two worksheets; distinguish between the two. They will be working first with the sheet that contains three figures; a cat, a man, and a flamingo. This sheet has its figures constructed to the exact scale of the seven tangram parts that they now possess. Their job is to recreate the three figures, remembering that all seven parts are used for each figure.

Notice that each figure has a small box near its title. This box is to be initialed by you when a student has created the appropriate worksheet figure. The student gets you to initial the box by raising his or her hand. You must state that it will be difficult for you to respond immediately to a raised hand; sometimes it will take a few minutes. So no one will sit idly with a raised hand, those who quickly finish a figure may proceed to another if the construction of the finished figure is recorded on the worksheet. The student records the figure by illustrating how the seven parts fit together. With a hand still raised and the figure recorded, the student is free to begin another figure.

The figures on the first worksheet are reproduced exactly to the scale of their seven tangram parts. Kids can superimpose the tangram parts onto the worksheet figures if they want. The figures on the second worksheet are not reproduced to exact scale. Hopefully, after the first worksheet has been completed, the kids will be able to transfer the construction techniques to the smaller-scale figures.

Again, for the second worksheet, it is imperative that the kids continue on while awaiting your approving initials.

You will notice that some figures have a square or a small triangle outlined. This is a hint.

Third and fourth graders show the best results if only the first worksheet is used. It is less complicated, and the figures are reproduced to scale. But the fifth through eighth graders are able to deal with the added complexities of smaller figures and proportions presented by the second worksheet. Have the fifth through eighth graders do both sheets.

If you can work variations into this lesson that will better adapt it to your style of teaching, do so.

I must stress again that the key to this lesson is making it clear that you can not provide immediate attention to every student. The kids must keep on working, with hands raised, after they have drawn the construction of the particular figure in question. Don't allow yourself to frantically chase hands. If you must repeatedly remind the class to work on, don't hesitate to do so!

References:
Lloyd, Sam: *The Eighth Book of Tan* ; Dover Publications, New York, 1968, paperback.

Read, Ronald C: *Tangrams: 330 Puzzles* ; Dover Publications, New York, 1965, paperback.

FOR ART IN TAN : 2 squares to each student.
FOR TANGRAMS : 1 square to each student initially.

Suggestion ~ Reproduce on **heavy** stock.

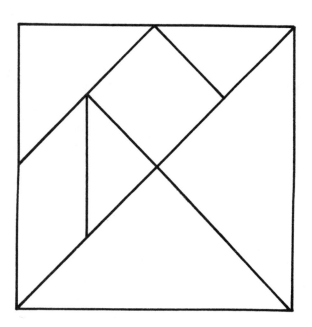 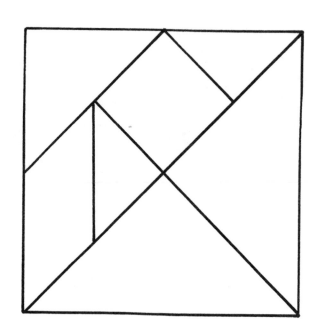

- - - - - - - - - - - - - - - - - - - - - - - - - - - - - - - - - - -

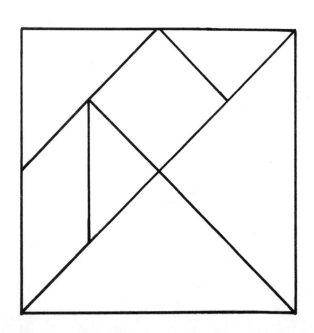 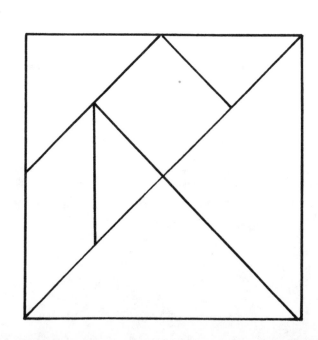

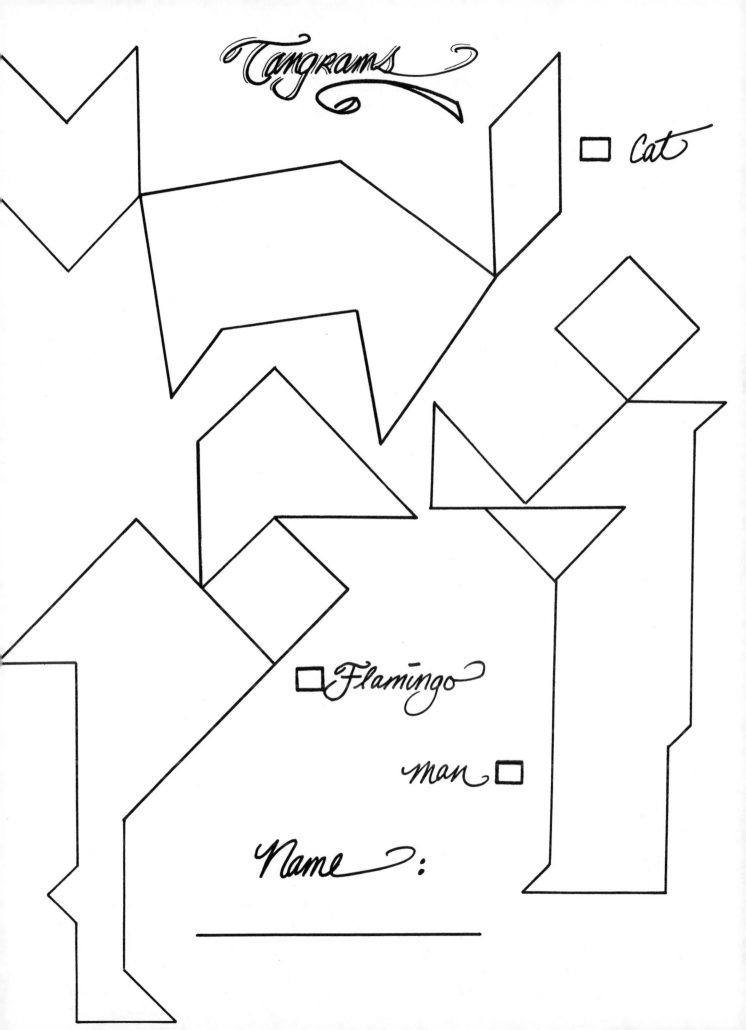

Tangrams

☐ Cat

☐ Flamingo

man ☐

Name :

_____

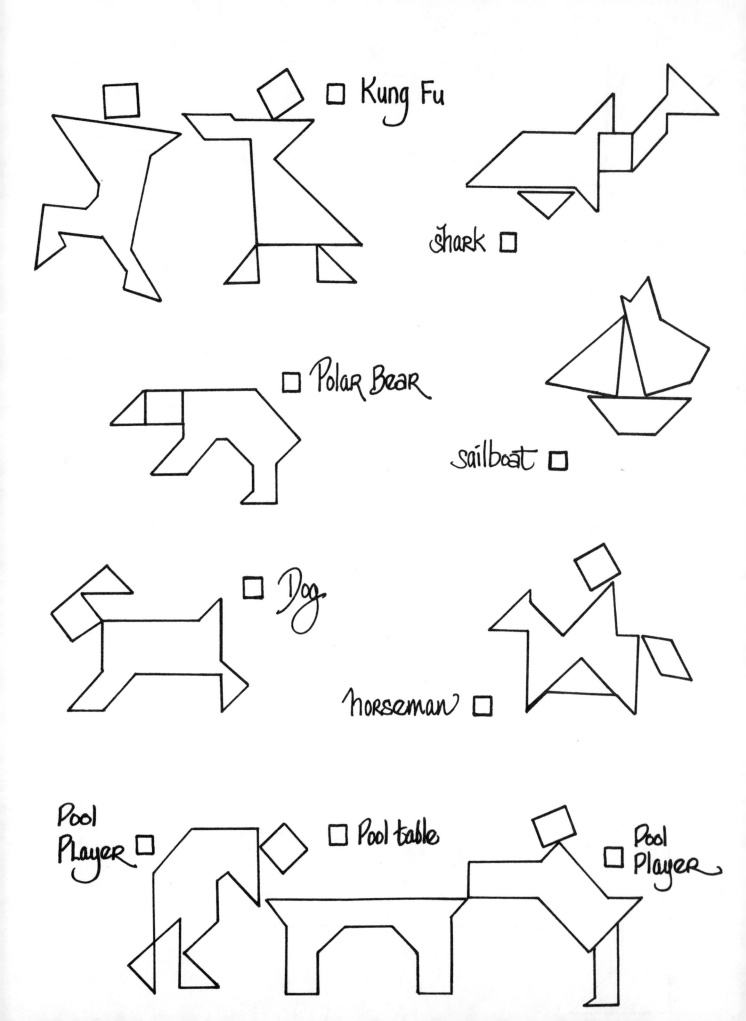

Kung Fu □

shark □

Polar Bear □

sailboat □

Dog □

horseman □

Pool Player □    □ Pool table    Pool Player □

# Pick a Number (2)

Here is a variation of *Pick a Number (1)* that incorporates division and multiplication.

STEPS :    (1.) Think of a number.
           (2.) Double that number.
           (3.) Add ___ (Select an even number -note: the answer will be one half of this number).
           (4.) Subtract the number you started with.

This variation is best done to a routine or a story.  For instance:

(1.) Think of a number of dollars -as many as you like.
(2.) Pretend that you barrow an equal amount from a rich friend.
     How many dollars do you have? (No, don't tell me, jot it down!)
(3.) I'm going to give you $___ (an even number).  Add this amount to your total.
(4.) All the money that you now have will be very useful if you're like me and owe money.
     So, pay half of your money to your creditors (indicate, if need be, that this means to divide by 2) .
(5.) Now repay your neighbor the amount you barrowed.
(6.) You should have $___ left  (one half of step 3).

You can really ham this one up.  And your story to accompany the operations can be really farfetched!  The wilder the story, the more the kids get sucked in.

As in *Pick a Number (1),*, welcome speculation as to a solution.

HE SAYS HE'S IN THE
PRIME OF HIS LIFE

# Cross + Numbers = Puzzles

Math places great emphasis on numbers and all-too-often underemphasizes the operations that affect those numbers. Here are three sets of puzzles that place strong emphasis on the operations affecting the numbers.

Master Sheet 1:    Concerned with the operations of addition and subtraction.

Master Sheet 2:    Concerned with all four operations: addition, subtraction, division, and multiplication.

Master Sheet 3:    All operations are given, but selected numbers are missing.

The difficulty level is, obviously, lower with Master Sheet 1 than 2 or 3. Depending upon the grade level and skill level, you can choose one of the three sheets to satisfy your teaching situation.

A lead-in to this exercise is very simple. Do a portion of one puzzle as an illustration. Explain that if there is doubt which operation to use, the old trial-and-error method will help resolve the doubt.

Start the kids off on the appropriate Master Sheet, then circulate among them, giving assistance. Your best assistance is illustrating, on a one-to-one basis, the trial-and-error method. Tell a questioning student to pick a sign for the first operation and try it out. For example, to solve-

| 4 | | 5 | | 3 | = | 3 |
|---|---|---|---|---|---|---|

(1.) Try subtracting: impossible
(2.) Try dividing: 5 won't divide into 4 evenly.
(3.) Try multiplication:

4 x 5 = 20, but there is nothing you can do to 20 with 3 to equal 3 $\longrightarrow$

$$20 - 3 \neq 3$$
$$20 \div 3 \neq 3$$
$$20 \times 3 \neq 3$$
$$20 + 3 \neq 3$$

Multiplication can be eliminated. And only one operation remains.

(4.) Addition: $4 + 5 = 9$. What operation can be preformed on 9 to equal 3?

$9 + 3 \neq 3$

$9 - 3 \neq 3$

$9 \times 3 \neq 3$          E U R E K A ! ! ! !

$9 \div 3 = 3$          $4 + 5 \div 3 = 3$

An excellent extension of this exercise is to have the kids make their own cross number puzzles. After you have given them time to work at least two of their Master Sheet puzzles, explain, illustrating on the board, how they can construct their own puzzles.

Illustrating upon the board is <u>very</u> important. If you impress upon them the logic of your example, you will make their creation process much simpler, and certainly less frustrating.

Your best preparation is to make (before the lesson) a puzzle of your own. You will quickly discover that the biggest problem is getting two columns to yield the same answer.

In presenting the exercise to the kids, include these procedures and instructions in you blackboard example:

(1.) Fill in the top horizontal row first, numbers and signs.
(2.) Fill in the far left column, numbers and signs.
(3.) Return to the horizontal rows, fill them in, but <u>do not</u> complete the bottom horizontal row. Leave it alone for now.
(4.) Return to the vertical columns. Fill them in, all b<u>ut</u> the signs of the far right vertical column.
(5.) The key to the puzzle by this procedure will be the bottom right square. It has to match the operations resulting form the horizontal and vertical computations.
(6.) Any adjustments to align lower right squares with the operations of the far right vertical column and the bottom horizontal row can usually be made by changing <u>signs</u> (not numbers) in the appropriate rows and columns.

To perform this lesson, it is <u>imperative</u> that you attempt to create your own puzzle before you explain any procedures to the kids. Your trial-and-error method will fully inform you of the <u>exact</u> problems the kids will face.

Kids are fascinated by their creations. When they have completed a puzzle-creating assignment, select three or four puzzles, copy them onto a ditto, reproduce the ditto, and give it to the kids the following day.

THERE GO THE
TIMES!

YEAH, THEY'RE
WORSE THAN
RABBITS!

**Top-left grid:**

| 2 |  | 3 |  | 2 | = | 3 |
|---|---|---|---|---|---|---|
|   |   |   |   |   |   |   |
| 3 |  | 5 |  | 6 | = | 2 |
|   |   |   |   |   |   |   |
| 2 |  | 6 |  | 7 | = | 1 |
| = |  | = |  | = |   | = |
| 3 |  | 2 |  | 1 | = | 4 |

Q: what number is another word for NO?

A: the number 9 *(written upside-down)*

**Top-right grid:**

| 8 |  | 1 |  | 4 | = | 5 |
|---|---|---|---|---|---|---|
|   |   |   |   |   |   |   |
| 1 |  | 4 |  | 2 | = | 3 |
|   |   |   |   |   |   |   |
| 4 |  | 2 |  | 1 | = | 5 |
| = |  | = |  | = |   | = |
| 5 |  | 3 |  | 5 | = | 7 |

# Cross Number Puzzles

## Fill in the signs + or − from top to bottom and from left to right

**Middle-right grid:**

| 3 |  | 2 |  | 7 | = | 8 |
|---|---|---|---|---|---|---|
|   |   |   |   |   |   |   |
| 8 |  | 7 |  | 9 | = | 10 |
|   |   |   |   |   |   |   |
| 6 |  | 4 |  | 2 | = | 0 |
| = |  | = |  | = |   | = |
| 5 |  | 5 |  | 18 | = | 18 |

**Bottom-left grid:**

| 4 |  | 5 |  | 8 | = | 1 |
|---|---|---|---|---|---|---|
|   |   |   |   |   |   |   |
| 7 |  | 7 |  | 10 | = | 4 |
|   |   |   |   |   |   |   |
| 3 |  | 1 |  | 9 | = | 11 |
| = |  | = |  | = |   | = |
| 18 |  | 11 |  | 9 | = | 16 |

Q: What is this?

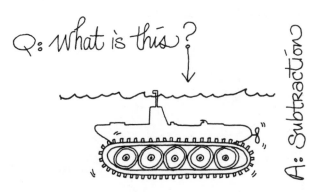

A: Subtraction

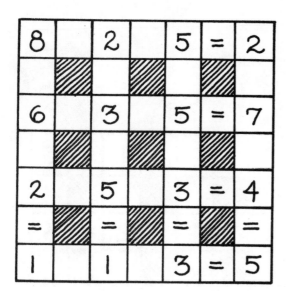

8 _ 2 _ 5 = 2
6 _ 3 _ 5 = 7
2 _ 5 _ 3 = 4
= _ = _ = = =
1 _ 1 _ 3 = 5

# CROSS NUMBER PUZZLES

FILL IN THE SIGNS +, −, ×, OR ÷ FROM LEFT TO RIGHT AND TOP TO BOTTOM.

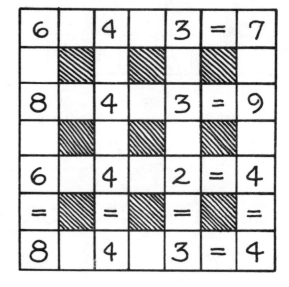

6 _ 4 _ 3 = 7
8 _ 4 _ 3 = 9
6 _ 4 _ 2 = 4
= _ = _ = = =
8 _ 4 _ 3 = 4

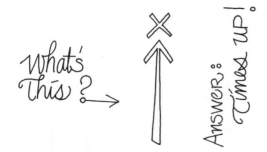

What's This? →

Answer: Times up!

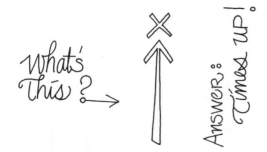

4 _ 5 _ 3 = 3
1 _ 8 _ 2 = 4
7 _ 4 _ 3 = 1
= _ = _ = = =
12 _ 9 _ 2 = 6

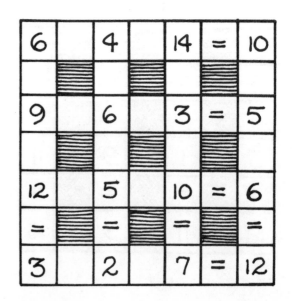

6 _ 4 _ 14 = 10
9 _ 6 _ 3 = 5
12 _ 5 _ 10 = 6
= _ = _ = = =
3 _ 2 _ 7 = 12

( ZERO RIDES AGAIN! )

# CROSS NUMBER PUZZLES

**Puzzle 1 (top left):**

| 6 | ÷ | 2 | × |  | = | 9 |
|---|---|---|---|---|---|---|
| × | ■ | − | ■ | × | ■ | − |
|  | ÷ |  | ÷ |  | = | 2 |
| − | ■ | ÷ | ■ | + | ■ | + |
| 6 | × | 1 | ÷ |  | = |  |
| = | ■ | = | ■ | = | ■ | = |
| 18 | × |  | − | 8 | = | 10 |

**Puzzle 2 (top right):**

| 3 | × |  | ÷ |  | = | 2 |
|---|---|---|---|---|---|---|
| × | ♥ | − | ♥ | + | ♥ | + |
| 2 | × |  | + | 4 | = |  |
| + | ♥ | × | ♥ | ÷ | ♥ | + |
|  | − | 6 | × |  | = | 2 |
| = | ♥ | = | ♥ | = | ♥ | = |
| 13 | + | 6 | − | 5 | = |  |

**Puzzle 3 (center):**

| 6 | × |  | + | 6 | = | 30 |
|---|---|---|---|---|---|---|
| ÷ | 🌷 | × | 🌷 | + | 🌷 | − |
| 3 | × |  | − |  | = |  |
| × | 🌷 | ÷ | 🌷 | − | 🌷 | × |
|  | + | 3 | ÷ |  | = | 3 |
| = | 🌷 | = | 🌷 | = | 🌷 | = |
| 18 | − |  | + | 13 | = | 15 |

**Puzzle 4 (bottom left):**

| 4 | × |  | + |  | = | 17 |
|---|---|---|---|---|---|---|
| ÷ | ✿ | × | ✿ | + | ✿ | + |
|  | × |  | ÷ |  | = | 8 |
| × | ✿ |  | ✿ |  | ✿ | − |
|  | ÷ |  | × |  | = |  |
| = | ✿ | = | ✿ | = | ✿ | = |
| 12 | + | 6 | − | 2 | = | 16 |

**Puzzle 5 (bottom right):**

| 60 | ÷ |  | × | 2 | = | 24 |
|---|---|---|---|---|---|---|
| ÷ | 🐦 | + | 🐦 | × | 🐦 | ÷ |
|  | − | 3 | ÷ |  | = |  |
| × | 🐦 | × | 🐦 | × | 🐦 | + |
|  | × |  | ÷ | 2 | = |  |
| = | 🐦 | = | 🐦 | = | 🐦 | = |
| 32 | + |  | ÷ |  | = | 48 |

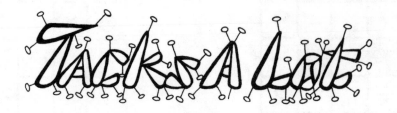

Here, indeed, is a very tacksing exercise. If you were given a varying number of squares and a varying number of thumbtacks, how could you mount the squares if the corners of each square must be fastened?

For example: Fasten 4 identical squares using 12 tacks.

One solution would be:

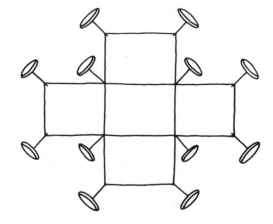

The corners may overlap for tacking as long as each corner is fastened.

This exercise works particularly well in small student groups. It seems that much of the confusion and frustration that occurs singularly is eliminated when several kids work together.

Merely go over the rules that are on the Master Sheet, then tackfully do the example on the board, and they're off.

I WONDER IF THE
KIDS WILL BE RATIONAL
WHEN THEY GROW UP

## RULES AND TACKTICS

(1) All squares must have a tack in each corner.

(2) Corners of squares can only overlap at the very edges.

(3) No square may be covered by another.

For Example – Fasten 2 squares
with 7 tacks . . . . . . . .

## PROBLEMS

(1) Fasten 3 squares with 8 tacks.
(2) Fasten 3 squares with 8 tacks that is different from number (1).
(3) Fasten 3 squares with 9 tacks.
(4) Fasten 3 squares with 10 tacks.
(5) Fasten 4 squares with 10 tacks.
(6) Fasten 4 squares with 9 tacks.
(7) Fasten 4 squares with 10 tacks that is different from number (5).
(8) Fasten 4 squares with 11 tacks.
(9) Fasten 4 squares with 12 tacks.
(10) Fasten 4 squares with 13 tacks.
(11) Fasten 5 squares using the greatest number of tacks possible.
(12) Fasten 5 squares using the fewest number of tacks possible.

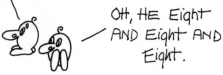

How DID HE GET SO FAT ?

OH, HE Eight AND Eight AND Eight.

# Mazes

Kids enjoy mazes. Mazes provide, due to the short time they take, an excellent means for a teacher to fill in small gaps of time between lessons. They are also a very convenient way to refocus the interest level of kids after a prolonged exercise or assignment.

Mazes are quite the publishing craze. The variations of subjects, formats, and designs span a wide gamut.

I usually select several mazes that can be placed on one sheet of paper for reproduction, then cut the page in half to provide two separate hand outs.

Collect mazes and maze publications which are engaging and which will provide kids with interest and intrigue.

MY, HE CERTAINLY IS
LOOKING SUCCESSFUL
THESE DAYS

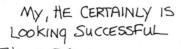

OH YES, HE WENT
INTO THE HULA HOOP
BUSINESS, ya know

# " I Have a Machine "

A short class-participation activity, that can be
supplemented with a worksheet, this involves
the patterned relationships of numbers. Draw
the following *machine* on the blackboard.

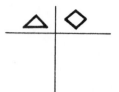

Explain that this machine takes in numbers ( ◇ )
and spews out answers ( △ ). For instance, if 2
goes into the machine, 5 comes out.

| △ | ◇ |
|---|---|
| 2 | 5 |

Ask kids for **in** numbers.

| △ | ◇ |
|---|---|
| 3 | 7 |
| 0 | 1 |
| 4 | 9 |

Student: 3        Teacher: If 3 goes in, 7 comes out.
Student: 0        Teacher: If 0 goes in, 1 comes out.
Student: 4        Teacher: If 4 goes in, 9 comes out.

Pretty soon someone will catch on and say, "All you're doing is multiply-
ing by two and adding one." Indicate that this is correct and illustrate by
way of a formula what is taking place.

$$2\triangle + 1 = \diamondsuit$$

The degree to which you complicate the formula should vary with the
group and level to which you are directing the lesson. With lower grades,
simple addition - subtraction will suffice:

$$\triangle + 2 = \diamondsuit \qquad \triangle - 1 = \diamondsuit \qquad \triangle + 7 = \diamondsuit$$

Older or more sophisticated groups will understand:

$$2\triangle = \diamondsuit \qquad 5\triangle + 1 = \diamondsuit$$
$$\triangle^2 = \diamondsuit \qquad 6\triangle + 6 = \diamondsuit$$

The more advanced the group, the greater complication you can involve
in the formula:

$$5\triangle - 7 = \diamond$$

$$\triangle^2 - 3 = \diamond$$

$$9\triangle + \triangle^2 = \diamond$$

$$8\triangle^2 = \diamond$$

To involve the kids further, have them devise their own formulas. Ask for a volunteer to work his or her formula on the board -as you have been doing- for class solution. BUT make sure the student shows you his or her formula before asking for **in** numbers. This will allow you to check the feasibility of the formula and to assure its correct application.

Further, you may even devise a worksheet as a follow up to the demonstration. Here is an excellent way to test paired relationships; give several pairs to establish the relationship. Then ask for completion:

| △ | ◇ |
|---|---|
| 3 | 10 |
| 8 | 25 |
| 4 | 13 |
| 7 | 22 |
| 9 | — |
| 6 | — |
| 2 | — |
| 0 | — |
| __ | 31 |
| __ | 16 |

Author-poet Kenneth Koch worked with the pupils of a Manhattan school to develop numerous approaches to children's poetry. His resulting first book, *Wishes Lies and Dreams* , records the efforts of his students.

The book explores many themes and techniques to enable children to write. One area is Wishes. An interesting variation of his classroom collaboration is very simply presented to students and usually provides great enjoyment.

**WISHES**

If you decide to use the book as the motivation for wish writing, brief mention of the book, the author, and the author's intention provides a good introduction. Explain that you would like to read some wishes from fourth, fifth, and sixth graders. Some of the wishes will be funny, some serious, some strange, and some downright corny. Students must remember that fourth graders don't think like sixth graders, and that ideas and sophistication vary considerably between grade levels.

Begin with a fourth grade example, follow with a fifth, and a sixth. A suggested sequence would be as follows:

> (1.) Grade 4, Lenora Calanni, page 77.
> (2.) Grade 4, Mayra Morales, page 81.
> (3.) Grade 5, Debbie Novitsky, page 83.
> (4.) Grade 6, Andrew Barish, page 85.

You may select more or different examples to fit. Your best signal as to the number of examples depends upon the composure of the class. Since you are presenting a complete lesson, bear in mind that overemphasis on examples detracts from the remaining portion of the lesson.

If you do not use the book and its examples as the instigation for writing wishes, the *I Wish...* Master Sheet will help provide the background necessary for student created wishes.

Whether or not you use the book, distribute of the *I Wish...* Master Sheet. These are actual student wishes compiled from *I Wish...* presentations which follow the format of this lesson.

After distributing the *I Wish...* Master Sheet, read the examples, pausing slightly to interject any comment. For example: "I wish I could tell someone how I feel about them."

Does that mean the all-too-often "I hate or dislike you" attitude? Or is this wish a very human approach to, "I feel something good toward you, but I find it hard to talk in such personal terms"?

These Master Sheet examples are selective, emphasizing humor largely, but also reflecting deeper thoughts.

After reading the Master Sheet, tell the kids to turn the sheet over and write five (or any number you desire) lines beginning with "I wish..." The wishes can be serious, humorous, or strange as they choose (as long as they're not mean toward anyone).

Allow suficient time. Collect the papers. Read the wishes back without mentioning names. Students want to hear what others write, so pace your reading to their attentiveness.

A few tips: having kids put their names on the papers often eliminates anonymous hate wishes. You need not read names. But remember, anonymity can often be a cover for vindictive or aggressive comments. You can always censor or delete inappropriate words or thoughts; it is up to you.

*Wishes, Lies, and Dreams: Teaching Children to Write Poetry* ; by Kenneth Koch and the Vintage Books/Chelsea House Publishers, 1970.

*I wish I had legs 10 feet long . . .*

name_____

I wish my sister would lose her voice.
I wish I could drive at my age.
I wish there weren't anything called cavities.
I wish we didn't have a mean bus driver.
I wish that I could tell someone how I feel about them.
I wish that our cooks would cook better.
I wish that Becky would stop wearing her glasses upside down.
I wish that love would fall right out of the sky on everyone.
I wish that my dad would become more modern.
I wish I were a piece of paper, then I would get written on.
I wish I had a pink-haired, blue-eyed guggle puss.
I wish there was no dog pound to rip off my dog.
I wish that my mom would quit yelling at me.
I wish I could be Rock Hudson so girls would chase me.
I wish girls were bald.
I wish that I was in kindergarden because Kathy and I would have a lot
        more fun again eating clay under desks.
I wish we had a soda fountain in the school.
I wish I didn't have to eat my eggs every morning.
I wish I had legs 10 feet long so I could run fast.
I wish Mr. T. would become a fig and jump in the nearest market of newtons.
I wish we never would have to get shots in the rumpus.
I wish that people would keep the world clean.
I wish I was an eagle with a man's brain.
I wish the Mayflower had sunk.
I wish that there was no such thing as asparagus, spinach, chow mein
        hot dogs, or squash.
I wish I could fly so my feet wouldn't hurt so much.
I wish a certain boy in our room would get transferred to Alaska.
I wish we could have school outside.
I wish I had something that made old people younger.
I wish I could write better than I do.
I wish everything for S.M.
I wish it were lunch so I could eat my heart out.
I wish starfish could sing, then they would be Ringo Star and sing, "I Want
        to Hold Your Hand."
I wish I had a pencil that did my work for me.
I wish I was a purple horse so I would be more noticeable.
I wish my dad wouldn't shave so I could use his whiskers for a paint brush.
I wish that I was a crossword puzzle so I could figure myself out.

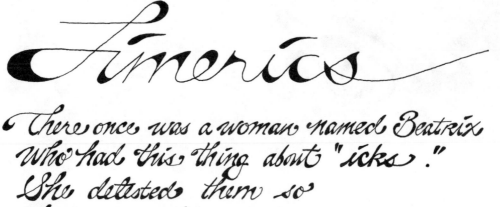

*There once was a woman named Beatrix,*
*Who had this thing about "icks."*
*She detested them so*
*That wouldn't you know*
*She even misspelled Limeric(k)s*

The limerick expresses a variety of sentiments, from the unprintable to the profound. Although traceable to the 18th century, the limerick was first popularized by Edward Lear in *The Book of Nonsense*, published in 1846.

Here is a lesson that begins with five lighthearted ditties.

BLAKE Read the limerick aloud to the kids and ask if there are patterns or characteristics that can be identified from the five lines. Establish that lines 1, 2, and 5 have rhyming last words, as do lines 3 and 4.

ZEKE and CLYDE Ask for some kids to read these limericks aloud. Reread them yourself, reinforcing the 1-2-5 and 3-4 rhyme. Ask if these limericks fit the same characteristics as did Blake. (Yes, they do.) These first three examples should be sufficient to establish the limerick in form and rhyme.

BRIAN There is something peculiar about "this fellow named Brian," you say. Something you can't sink your teeth into. How about the rhyming scheme? What's this 'fion' business? There is no such word as 'fion.' What does fion really mean? (Fine.) Why didn't the author use fine instead of fion? (It wouldn't have rhymed.) Make sure the kids understand this 'poetic license.'

THE GNU The "gnu in the zoo" has two phonetic variations. The key words in this limerick are 'gnu' and 'gnobody.'

The reading of this limerick depends upon how you pronounce 'gnu' - silent 'g' or sounded 'g.' What is a gnu anyway? (Right, an African buffalo, also known as a wildebeast.)

If the 'g' is properly left unpronounced ('new') what happens to that 'gnobody' in the last line? (It's unpronounced, too.)

If the 'g' is pronounced in gnu, what pronunciation does 'gnobody' take? (Right, the 'g' is also pronounced.) It makes for a pleasant alliterative sequence when followed by gnu ('g' pronounced).

<u>WRITING A FIFTH LINE</u>  At the bottom of the Master Sheet are three limericks that are without fifth lines.

Begin with one, perhaps the far left one. Read it aloud. Explain that they must write a fifth line. What words will the fifth line have to rhyme with? (That's right, Billy and Philly.) The fifth line rhyme might be 'silly', 'hillbilly', 'Milly', 'Willy', etc. Allow time for the composition of the fifth line. Ask for volunteers to read the entire limerick, inserting their fifth line.

Finish the other two incomplete limericks in the same manner.

If the class is interested enough at that point, you might be able to compose a class limerick. Determine a subject. For instance, I remember one class which picked their principal to compose a limerick about. Luckily the kids really liked their principal. Unfortunately though, for me, some little darling immediately dashed off after the limerick had been composed to present the principal with the fresh copy.

————

Say, did ya hear? I sold my Donut Shop.
No, Really? Why'd ya do that?
Oh, I got tired of the whole business.

o,o!

A careless explorer named Blake
Fell into a tropical lake.
Said a fat alligator
A few minutes later,
" Very nice, but I still prefer steak. "

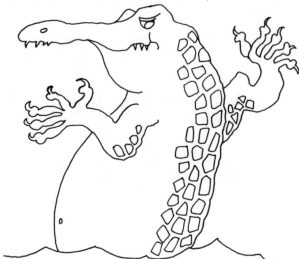

A famous bullfighter named Zeke
Pleased the crowds with his casual technique.
Each time he was gored
He just acted bored,
Pausing only to plug up the leak.

A young rock - and - roller named Clyde
Always kept his guitar by his side ;
All night he kept strumming
And never stopped humming ,
'Til he ran out of rhythm and died.

There once was a fellow named Brian
Who was bitten one day by a lion.
He went on the prowl
And he started to growl,
But other than that he's just fion.

There once was a gnu in the zoo
Who tired of the same daily view.
To seek a new sight
He stole out one night —
But where he went gnobody gnu !

Did you ever hear about Billy
A smart young boy from Philly ?
Who wore a wig
And danced the jig
_____ .

If you want to go to the moon
And you hope to go quite soon
Then you must face
That to travel in space
_____ .

There once was a sailor named Fred
Whose feet always stuck out of bed ;
Said the fellow below
As he stared at Fred's toe,
_____ .

Bairnard is a
spoof that is a good vehi
cle for a creative writing lesso
n.  The kids should listen 'carrotfu
lly' to the episode — *BAIRNARD: The
Carrot Crusader  *OR*  "Why are my car
rots yellow and mushy ? "*  From your reading
and from the Master Sheet that you will distribute
prior to the reading, the kids will usually come to rega
rd ol' Bairnard rather fondly.  If they understand the pu
ns in the script, all the better for them. In any event, use
the episode and the Master Sheet to lay the basis for an in-cla
ss asingnment.  Have them compose a further episode involving
Bairnard.   The tenor of the initial episode and any ideas that you
can evoke about Barinard will assist in making the creation of anot
her episode easier for the kids.  There will always be those who com
plain or those who want you to tell them what to write.   Try to build
Bairnard up enough so they can venture upon their own episode as
smoothly as possible.  And wherever you can, let your fantasies be
your guide.

# BAIRNARD

# Bairnard: The Carrot Crusader or "Why are my carrots yellow & mushy?"

THIS is Bairnard. We are seeing Bairnard at one of his strange moments. Bairnard never really got over his childhood Superman phase. He has, though I don't think he'd admit it, always kept it fondly in his recollections. That was....UNTIL RECENTLY.

Bairnard is now, at the age of 43, going through what he calls his Rabbit Man stage -he says it "really suits" him. Bairnard could never tidily fit into a Superman outfit or a Captain America costume. So he did the next best thing; he created his own outfit.

Does Bairnard stop crime? Does Bairnard fight injustice? Does Bairnard battle violence? Of course not. Look at that face! Bairnard can't see too well, and can you imagine how it is for him behind that mask, having to look out? Bairnard can't move too fast. Look at those rabbit footsies. They're all Bairnard's. Look at those paws. Bairnard couldn't put a penny in a gumball machine.

"What," I can hear you say, "is it with this oversized carrot freak?" Let's find out exactly what is behind that powder puff tail and under those anemic ears.

I must explain that I am Bairnard's closest friend. And from what he has told me and what I have heard from other sources, Bairnard started this hubbub about six weeks ago.

ONE DAY...Usda Butcher was working away, as usual, in the same small corner market that he had run everyday for 32 years. His morning had been like any typical weekday morning: rolling out the awning, sweeping the floors, and cleaning the plate glass windows. With these chores done, USDA had turned to his butcher blook and the job of cutting a mound of newly arrived chickens that were part of his weekly special. Mind you, cutting capon chickens is a serious matter to Usda; although, I must admit, he has been heard to cackle, "Boy, what a chicken job." Anyway, Usda had always undertaken great mental preparation before he began this precise chore. And he was so deeply concerned with his capons that it wasn't until after our carrot crusader had entered the market that Usda sensed something wrong. Bairnard had hopped in past the check-out counter. He hesitated before the shelves of canned vegetables and wiggled his nose before the Creamed Carrots. But then he continued on back to the fresh vegetable section. He passed the apples neatly stacked in a pyramid. He hopped around the scale that hung from the ceiling. And there, next to the sign marked bananas, was what he had come to capture.

It was just as Bairnard had passed the hanging scale that Usda saw him. Usda stood amazed. Quickly Bairnard gathered the choicest of plunder. Then he suddenly pawed his whiskers and hopped toward the door. By the time Bairnard reached the door, Usda had stepped from behind the cutting block.

Bairnard may look big and awkward. But if there is one thing that Bairnard can do, it's "hop to it" -so he told me with a twitch of his nose and a gleam in his eyes.

Usda gazed in bewilderment as he stood in the doorway. Hat in hand, he scratched his head and muttered over and over, "Aw, bananas." How was he going to explain this: a big rabbit stealing his bananas?

Meanwhile Bairnard was high-tailing it toward home. Can you imagine the sight Bairnard would have made to anyone unfortunate enough to see him? He ran clutching his goods like a bear hugging a tree. His large feet did not make quite the sound that you would expect a fast moving rabbit to make. They sounded more like horse hooves upon a cobblestone road.

By the time Bairnard reached home, he was exhausted. He immediately removed his rabbit-head. And with a sigh he adjusted his glasses, for they had fallen off his nose. Had they not fallen, they still would have been of little use, for they were all fogged up. It seems Bairnard had only put two small holes in his rabbit-head. And those holes were only to see out of. Really, Bairnard was lucky to have seen anything, under the circumstances.

Bairnard neatly removed his suit. He placed it on a hanger and hung it in a special, secret place in his closet. Leaving his captured goods on the dining room table, Bairnard quickly changed into his everyday sports clothes. He had carefully picked these clothes so as to keep with the latest style. The Hawaiian print shirt was neatly pressed. The plaid Bermuda shorts and knee-length socks had been specially ordered. And his laced leather boots were shined with the greatest of care.

Bairnard smiled one of his strange and happy smiles as he thought back on his adventure. And as he watered his indoor plants, that smile became broader. And as he dusted the mantel-piece, his smile turned into a chuckle. And before he knew it, Bairnard was smiling, chuckling, and running around with delight. Boy, he really had put one over on old Usda!

Bairnard stopped before the dining room table. He took one of the carrots from the bunch. It did look a little pale, much too much on the yellowish side for a ripe carrot. And when he bit into it, it was a bit mushy. But all the same, Bairnard was delighted. He finally settled himself into his favorite armchair and fell asleep. After all, he did deserve a nap after what he had just accomplished.

Students enjoy word searches, particularly when they have some direct association with the words involved. Commercial word search publications, to numerous and obscure to list here, are present at most newstands or magazine racks. But these commercial publications too often present mundane words and topics with which students have little or no interest. Bearing the commercial pulp in mind, here are several searches that engage most age groups.

(1.) The United States

(2.) The State Capitols

(3.) Pigskin Parade

(4.) National/American League Baseball Teams

(5.) Presidents of the United States

The boys are immediately taken by the very mention of sports, thus the inclusion of two such searches is directly aimed at them.

The United States and The State Capitols are, of course, a sly way to reinforce student knowledge of the fifty states.

Student, also, revel in making their own word searches. Provide them with suitable words (ah, the ol' spelling list!) and they will provide suitable searches. Selected searches can be duplicated by the teacher and returned to the students for solution (especially good for weekly spelling lists, or review lists, or special topics).

## A STORY

Once upon a time some kids saw that I was trying to create a word search. They wanted to try it, so to be rid of them while I did my work, I gave each a piece of quarter-inch graph paper. They took it upon themselves to construct a word search on a subject of their choosing. One chose the presidents of the United States; one chose major rivers of the United States; one decided to write everyone's last name into a search; and others chose subjects that varied from animals to cars. The most important feature of the whole occurance was that they took it upon themselves to use resource materials to find out about their respective topics.

Certainly they did not learn everything about their chosen topic in the process of their research, but they were sparked into using resource materials. And to my knowledge, they have been happily word searching ever after.

# THE UNITED STATES

The names of the 50 United States can be found within this word search.
The names are written forwards, backwards, up, down and diagon**ally.**

```
T  U  C  I  T  C  E  N  N  O  C  A  F  R  I  C  A  Z  I  G  G  Y
E  U  R  O  P  E  I  X  V  E  R  M  O  N  T  D  U  E  M  E  A  K
A  R  I  Z  O  N  A  I  N  I  G  R  I  V  T  S  E  W  I  O  N  C
A  I  N  R  O  F  I  L  A  C  H  I  N  A  M  S  M  A  N  R  A  U
N  O  T  G  N  I  H  S  A  W  I  N  A  G  S  O  E  D  N  G  I  T
S  O  U  T  H  D  A  K  O  T  A  N  E  E  J  K  X  I  E  I  S  N
M  A  R  Y  L  A  N  D  N  P  I  H  N  W  O  N  I  R  S  A  I  E
O  R  U  T  A  H  A  T  U  L  F  N  E  E  J  X  C  O  O  W  U  K
A  K  A  O  H  O  A  W  O  I  E  H  T  B  V  E  O  L  T  S  O  T
K  R  L  S  U  C  S  R  D  T  C  H  I  L  E  A  R  F  A  C  L  S
S  O  A  A  I  N  A  V  L  Y  S  N  N  E  P  O  D  S  Z  A  P  D
A  Y  S  X  H  C  S  R  N  A  G  I  H  C  I  M  N  A  E  J  K  R
R  W  K  E  H  O  W  Y  O  M  I  N  G  V  O  A  C  A  B  Y  E  H
B  E  A  T  I  E  M  O  H  L  O  O  K  I  K  L  D  H  I  E  O  O
E  N  U  R  A  L  S  A  I  O  I  M  O  R  E  A  T  E  N  A  D  D
N  O  R  T  H  D  A  K  O  T  A  N  A  G  V  B  N  I  D  P  A  E
S  R  I  R  U  O  S  S  I  M  T  S  A  I  G  A  A  S  I  E  R  D
N  E  W  H  A  M  P  S  H  I  R  E  F  N  H  M  O  E  A  Z  O  N
O  G  I  P  P  I  S  S  I  S  S  I  M  I  J  A  L  M  N  S  L  A
W  O  C  I  X  E  M  W  E  N  D  E  L  A  W  A  R  E  A  T  O  L
A  N  A  T  N  O  M  O  O  S  E  N  I  S  N  O  C  S  I  W  C  S
S  T  T  E  S  U  H  C  A  S  S  A  M  X  S  I  O  N  I  L  L  I
```

Alabama
Alaska
Arizona
Arkansas
California
Colorado
Connecticut
Deleware
Florida
Georgia
Hawaii
Idaho
Illinois
Indiana
Iowa
Kansas
Kentucky
Louisiana
Maine
Maryland
Massachusetts
Michigan
Minnesota
Mississippi
Missouri
Montana
Nebraska
Nevada
New Hampshire
New Jersey
New Mexico
New York
North Carolina
North Dakota
Ohio
Oklahoma
Oregon
Pennsylvania
Rhode Island
South Carolina
South Dakota
Tennessee
Texas
Utah
Vermont
Virginia
Washington
West Virginia
Wisconsin
Wyoming

# STATE CAPITALS

The state capitals of the 50 United States are found in this Word Search.
The names of the capitals are written forwards, backwards, up, down, and diagonally.

```
E     Y E R R E I P I N D I A N A P O L I S
C E   N T   J E F F E R S O N C I T Y       P
N A S A   I         S P R I N G F I E L D H A
E K   S D   C A N A D A A N     A         A   I
D E C H A R L E S T O N I L T         R D     N
I P   V   H O   K   S S A N B       T   E B A
V O   I     A   C   A N U A U     A F   J S I I
O T   L       L N A L L B C S O N     A M S B
R R A L E I G H L O T S     M R T     Y C O M M
P H O E N I X       A C   A D U A I       K I A U
O       K C O R E L T T I L Y L M N S N R L
    K M G B A T O N R O U G E T S O E O E C O
    Y L O R F H O N O L U L U I I   C N S K C
    R   A N U R D E N V E R   C L U A P T S
J E   E H T B A U G U S T A N O B O S T O N
U M L S   O P S N I T A L Y O P     A R R O
N O S I D A M E I K A S I A S A     N E E L
E G A O N     A L R F       R N     T N V Y
A T L B   C     C I R U     A N     A T O M
U N E       O     I E A R   C A     F O D P
    O M   A N E L E H T R H T       E N   I
    M   C H E Y E N N E Y   R I C H M O N D A
```

Alabama - MONTGOMERY
Alaska - JUNEAU
Arizona - PHOENIX
Arkansas - LITTLE ROCK
California - SACRAMENTO
Colorado - DENVER
Connecticut - HARTFORD
Deleware - DOVER
Florida - TALLAHASSEE
Georgia - ATLANTA
Hawaii - HONOLULU
Idaho - BOISE
Illinois - SPRINGFIELD
Indiana - INDIANAPOLIS
Iowa - DES MOINES
Kansas - TOPEKA
Kentucky - FRANKFURT
Louisiana - BATON ROUGE
Maine - AUGUSTA
Maryland - ANNAPOLIS
Massachusetts - BOSTON
Michigan - LANSING
Minnesota - ST. PAUL
Mississippi - JACKSON
Missouri - JEFFERSON CITY
Montana - HELENA
Nebraska - LINCOLN
Nevada - CARSON CITY
New Hampshire - CONCORD
New Jersey - TRENTON
New Mexico - SANTE FE
New York - ALBANY
North Carolina - RALEIGH
North Dakota - BISMARCK
Ohio - COLUMBIA
Oklahoma - OKLAHOMA CITY
Oregon - SALEM
Pennsylvania - HARRISBURG
Rhode Island - PROVIDENCE
South Carolina - COLUMBIA
South Dakota - PIERRE
Tennessee - NASHVILLE
Texas - AUSTIN
Utah - SALT LAKE CITY
Vermont - MONTPELIER
Virginia - RICHMOND
Washington - OLYMPIA
West Virginia - CHARLESTON
Wisconsin - MADISON
Wyoming - CHEYENNE

# PIGSKIN PARADE

The team names of the 28 National and American Football League
teams are in this Word Search.  Can you find them all?

```
B  S  E  A  H  A  W  K  S  P  A  D  R  E  S
U  S  T  S  O  L  P  N  F  R  S  L  L  I  B
C  T  S  L  N  L  O  A  S  O  S  T  M  D  S
C  N  T  E  I  I  L  C  C  S  T  S  R  M  R
A  I  S  O  L  C  K  N  P  K  E  P  A  D  E
N  A  N  E  O  G  O  S  P  S  E  R  N  O  G
E  S  S  N  S  R  A  A  D  T  L  R  C  S  R
E  S  S  T  B  R  T  E  I  E  E  A  S  V  A
R  O  E  T  S  R  E  D  I  A  R  N  I  T  H
S  J  N  P  I  B  G  N  A  D  S  K  S  S  C
T  P  S  O  S  R  E  L  I  O  I  N  O  O  R
W  A  T  N  O  S  S  N  E  N  I  R  W  A  S
I  S  L  S  T  N  A  I  G  H  Y  B  T  F  M
N  O  S  T  W  L  R  S  P  A  O  T  E  S  E
S  T  C  O  S  E  E  L  E  Y  L  I  R  N  T
V  S  R  A  E  B  O  R  S  T  H  S  S  O  S
W  B  R  P  O  D  O  E  R  C  S  S  L  O  F
```

## NATIONAL LEAGUE

Dallas COWBOYS
New York GIANTS
Philadelphia EAGLES
Phoenix CARDINALS
Washington REDSKINS
Chicago BEARS
Detroit LIONS
Green Bay PACKERS
Minnesota VIKINGS
Atlanta FALCONS
Los Angeles RAMS
New Orleans SAINTS
San Francisco FORTY-NINERS
Tampa Bay BUCCANEERS

## AMERICAN LEAGUE

Indianapolis COLTS
New England PATRIOTS
Buffalo BILLS
Miami DOLPHINS
New York JETS
Cincinnati BENGALS
Cleveland BROWNS
Houston OILERS
Pittsburgh STEELERS
Denver BRONCOS
Kansas City CHIEFS
Los Angeles RAIDERS
San Diego CHARGERS
Seattle SEAHAWKS

# NATIONAL/AMERICAN LEAGUE BASEBALL TEAMS

National and American League baseball teams can be found in this word search.
There are also a number of other baseball terms and postions.  Can you find them?

```
A  S  T  R  O  N  A  U  T  S  R  E  H  C  T  A  C  S
S  N  A  I  D  N  I  O  L  S  F  Z  N  X  B  A  M  R
C  L  U  B  A  Q  L  A  T  N  A  R  A  T  A  T  E  E
A  I  B  A  M  S  Y  E  P  I  R  A  T  E  S  H  W  N
R  D  R  N  E  O  P  A  F  W  O  F  I  S  E  L  H  I
D  N  E  G  R  W  T  O  N  T  U  I  O  O  B  E  I  R
I  O  W  E  I  B  I  K  E  K  T  S  N  C  A  T  T  A
N  C  E  L  C  X  G  Z  A  P  E  N  A  C  L  I  E  M
A  E  R  S  A  E  E  Y  O  Y  O  E  L  E  L  C  S  S
L  S  S  T  N  X  R  A  N  G  E  R  S  R  U  S  O  Y
S  E  R  D  A  P  S  O  U  P  I  D  E  R  S  O  X  A
G  I  F  T  Z  O  S  H  O  R  T  A  D  R  I  H  T  J
E  B  A  T  V  S  F  I  R  S  T  Z  N  A  I  L  H  E
L  P  H  I  L  L  I  E  S  O  S  B  S  T  E  M  S  U
D  R  E  T  N  E  C  Q  U  B  R  A  V  E  S  V  I  L
E  D  O  D  G  E  R  S  U  P  I  T  C  H  E  R  R  B
R  L  E  A  G  U  E  C  A  T  S  E  L  O  I  R  O  Z
```

## National League

Chicago CUBS
New York METS
Montreal EXPOS
Pittsburgh PIRATES
Philadelphia PHILLIES
St. Louis CARDINALS

San Francisco GIANTS
Houston ASTRONAUTS
Cincinnati RED LEGS
Los Angeles DODGERS
Atlanta BRAVES
San Diego PADRES

## American League

Texas RANGERS
Detroit TIGERS
Boston RED SOX
Minnesota TWINS
New York YANKEES
Baltimore ORIOLES
Seattle Mariners

Milwaukee BREWERS
Cleveland INDIANS
Chicago WHITE SOX
California ANGELS
Oakland ATHLETICS
Kansas City ROYALS
Toranto BLUE JAYS

# PRESIDENTS OF THE UNITED STATES

Here are the names of 40 Presidents of the United States.

```
S M A D A N H O J B U C H A N A N P I E J
G A R F I E L D U S A N O S R E F F E J O
L J W A S H I N G T O N L U C K Y F G T R
O O N I X O N V Y N K A I S T A R O D B E
P H O E L O U L O E C G N D Y A A O I L T
Z N S O D L E S N W X E C L N T F T L Y R
N Q I R E R I N I C K R O K O R T T O N A
O U R N L D E A E R O M L L I F F B O D C
S I R O A D U P M A N I N D U M H Y C O T
N N A M Y J A C K H N S M I T H S R A N G
H C H A R D I N G D H O O V E R U J A J K
O Y N T I O U S R I L A X L E H B R D O D
J A I G A L E O D O E P R Q T R G U M H N
W D M B C Y O D T H J E C R E I P N C N A
E A A D A S L H P R N G A V I W O R K S L
R M J H E A T O V T U F O R D S S L I O E
D S N V A N B U R E N M O L L Y O C N N V
N K E I S E N H O W E R A I P P I N L G E
A L B C C N O S K C A J W N Q U I T E Z L
T L E V E S O O R E R O D O E H T X Y Q C
```

WASHINGTON
JOHN ADAMS
JEFFERSON
MADISON
MONROE
JOHN QUINCY ADAMS
JACKSON
VAN BUREN
WILLIAM H. HARRISON
TYLER
POLK
TAYLOR
FILLMORE

PIERCE
BUCHANAN
LINCOLN
ANDREW JOHNSON
GRANT
HAYES
GARFIELD
ARTHUR
CLEVELAND
BENJAMIN HARRISON
MC KINLEY
THEODORE ROOSEVELT
TAFT
WILSON

HARDING
COOLIDGE
HOOVER
FRANKLIN D.  ROOSEVELT
TRUMAN
EISENHOWER
KENNEDY
LYNDON JOHNSON
NIXON
FORD
CARTER
REGAN
BUSH

# Them Poems

If you have read Mason Williams' *The Mason Williams Reading Matter* or *Flavors*, you have become pleasantly aware of Them Poems. Them Poems portray the true and forever essence of such American stalwarts as Lunch Toters, Sand Pickers, Tummy Gummers, Toad Suckers, and Dog Kickers.

These formula poems are engaging creations that combine strange characters and doin's. The tone is humorous and the grammar atrocious. They are a folksy expression of downhome people. And they provide an excellent lesson that combines a number of talents: rhyming, cadence, awareness of dialect, and humor.

Your best preparation is, first, to read all of the Thems Poems in both publications. Several are risque, but again depending upon the class level and composure, most are presentable to the kids. All the poems are a variation of a standard formula. The formula, reproduced for the Master Sheet, will provide the format from which the kids will create their own Them Poems.

You will need to set the tone of these poems for the kids. I often parallel the tone to the Hee-Haw T.V. show. I indicate that these poems have the linguistic overtones of mountain or hillbilly people. In this way, you can read several Them Poems in a country tone and the language characteristics such as 'them' for 'those' or dropping the 'g' in 'ing' word forms will be reinforced.

You can introduce the kids to Them Poems in different ways. You can just read several. Or you can pick out several, type those selections on a ditto (possibly select Lunch Toters, Tummy Gummers, and Sand Pickers), hand out the ditto, and read the selections to the class. This approach works well, for it allows the kids to see the style and the layout of the poems, while hearing your dialect and oral reading. When you read a poem, lapse as fully as possible into a twangy, downhome dialect. It works great!

Included for further emphasis are four student created Them Poems. Reading these will further reinforce rhyming and cadence patterns for the kids.

**Gittin' Them Poem Writers to Write**

Pass out the Your Them Poem Master Sheet.

Explain the Master Sheet as follows:

<u>Title</u>: The title, and consequently the poem subject, has to be in two parts. Some kids will probably say that they can't think of a subject. So....here is a sampling of subjects from kid- written Them Poems.

| | |
|---|---|
| Bug Eaters | Hat Snatchers |
| Show Snatchers | Paper Eaters |
| School Learners | Spider Smashers |
| Nose Pickers | Money Hoggers |
| Knife Throwers | Hair Pullers |
| Frog Lickers | Bath Takers |
| Hitch Hikers | Bean Pickers |
| Snail Eaters | Roller Skaters |
| Berry Pickers | Bike Riders |

<u>Them Subject:</u> Must be a two-part subject.

<u> X :</u> Indicate the rhyming scheme, the last word in the second and fourth sentence of each verse.

<u>2nd Word of Subject + 'in:</u> Take the second word from the subject, drop 'ers' and add 'in'. For instance, toters becomes totin', gummers becomes gummin', and pickers becomes pickin'.

<u>2 Word Description:</u> A two-word adjective that describes the Them subject. For instance:

> ...long-stringy Bean Pickers...
> ...tub-sittin' Bath Takers...
> ...mighty-awkward Roller Skaters...

I usually give the kids time to write their own poems. I circulate, trying to help those who still need a subject or those who have rhyming problems. Kids will just pester you unmercifully to do their work for them. But this is typical for many creative writing assignments.

After a period, I allow those who are willing to read their poems aloud. But in any event, you have to encourage, coax, cajole, and praise.

As with any lesson, be attentive to your initial presentation and incorporate any variations that will better suit your future lessons.

By Mason Williams:

*The Mason Williams Reading Matter* ; Doubleday and Company, New York, paperback, 1969.

*Flavors* ; Doubleday and Company, New Yourk, paperback, 1970.

## Them Dirty Streakers

How about them Dirty Streakers,
Ain't they cool?
Showin' off they bods,
Streakin' through the school.

Streakin' down the alley,
Streakin' in the room,
Passin' by the church,
Streakin' on a broom.

Look at them Dirty Streakers,
Makin' all the news.
Streakin' all around,
In they tenny shoes.

Them mighty-fast Dirty Streakers,
Think it's fun,
Runnin' down the street,
Showin' off they buns.

How to be a Dirty Streaker?
Don't have a fit,
Find yourself a street,
Haul off and streak it!

## Them Roller Skaters

How about them Roller Skaters,
Ain't they neat?
Skatin' all around,
Fallin' on they seat.

Look at them Skaters,
Skatin' in the town,
Skatin' in the alley,
Fallin' right down.

Look at them Roller Skaters,
Ain't they cool?
Skatin' in they underwear,
Lookin' like a fool.

Them mighty-awkward Roller Skaters,
A skatin' on the farm,
Skatin' in they pastures,
And skatin' 'round they barn.

How to be a Roller Skater?
Anyone can do it,
It ain't hard,
If ya stick to it.

## Them Bean Pickers

How about them Bean Pickers,
Ain't they cool ?
Runnin' all around,
Actin' like fools.

Pickin' them lima beans,
Pickin' them fast,
Pickin' all day,
While they last.

Look at them Bean Pickers,
Ain't they funny,
Pickin' them beans,
Makin' lots a money.

Them long-stringy Bean Pickers,
Ain't they wise ?
Pickin' them beans,
No madder what size.

How to be a Bean Picker ?
It's mighty easy.
Just bean yourself down,
And they'll come easy.

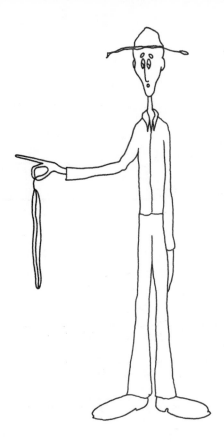

## Them Bath Takers

How about them Bath Takers,
Ain't they wet ?
Scrubin' so hard,
It makes them sweat.

Scrubin' them elbows,
Scrubin' them toes,
Some use a bristle brush,
Some use they nose.

Look at them Bath Takers,
Ain't they dumb ?
Scrubin' they fingers,
Scrubin' they thumbs.

Them tub-sittin' Bath Takers,
Ain't they a blast ?
Sittin' all day,
While they suds last.

How to be a Bath Taker ?
Don't need a ticket.
Jest find yourself a bath tub,
Skooch down and take it.

NAME_____

( *title* ) THEM_____

How about them_____ _____,
                      ( *Them  Subject* )
Ain't they_____?
                  *x*

_____,

_____.
               *x*

_____,
 ( *2ⁿᵈ word of subject + 'in'* )

_____,
 ( *2ⁿᵈ word of subject + 'in'* )  *x*

_____,
 ( *2ⁿᵈ word of subject + 'in'* )

_____.
               *x*

Look at them _____ _____,
                    ( *Them  Subject* )

_____?
               *x*

_____,

_____.
               *x*

Them _____ _____.
     ( *2 word description* )        ( *Them  Subject* )

_____?
               *x*

_____,

_____.
               *x*

How to be a _____ _____?
               ( *Them  Subject* )

_____.
               *x*

_____,

_____.
               *x*

# Scrambled Eggs

When words are grouped to represent a desired thought, they follow certain patterns of grammatical construction. These patterns are often intuitively understood, finding repeated examples in the banter of common speech. Kids often become confused about these patterns when they are required to identify them with such foreign labels as subject, verb, or object. The detection equipment that they have developed to explain the processes of language don't always jive with the many labels and explanations provided by state adopted language texts.

Here is a language exercise that uses a student's intuitive knowledge to generate a sentence from a jumble of words. The jumbled sentences begin simply, but progress into longer and more intricate sentences toward the end.

Sometimes sentences have more than one interpretation, owing to an interchange of similar words. For example, Sentence 4 could be writen as:

> The cat ran after the mouse.

> or

> The mouse ran after the cat.

Sentence 19 could be written:

> The baby chickens took care of the little children

> or

> The little children took care of the baby chickens.

Kids will usually delight in being able to interpret sentences as they see fit. The mouse ran after the cat, because of its comical nature is preferred over the typical and more realistic, The cat ran after the mouse. Point this

85

out by saying as long as the sentences are grammatically correct, the nonsense or fantasy constructions (as: The mouse ran after the cat.) are acceptable.

Circulate when the kids are working. Occasionally you might draw class attention to a particular sentence that sense doesn't make.

# Scrambled Eggs

Name _____

Rewrite the following sentences so they make sense. Each sentence starts with the <u>underlined</u> word.

1. to <u>Jane</u> mother store for went the.

2. likes play <u>Jack</u> to ball.

3. doll has <u>Susan</u> new a.

4. after cat mouse the ran <u>The</u>.

5. sunny <u>Today</u> day is a.

6. yard rake will the <u>Father</u>.

7. like <u>Birds</u> sing to.

8. winter falls in <u>Snow</u> the.

9. ears have big <u>Elephants</u>.

10. night shines at <u>The</u> moon.

11. climbed a boys <u>The</u> tree.

12. is a pig <u>A</u> animal farm.

13. the sells <u>She</u> by seashore seashells.

14. trees grow on <u>Apples</u>.

15. color needed crayons <u>The</u> students to.

16. <u>The</u> horse jumped from his prince young.

17. vegetables <u>The</u> truck with the loaded farmer.

18. paper or pencil <u>We</u> could not find the.

19. <u>The</u> baby chickens took care of the little children.

20. <u>A</u> cow is a calf baby.

21. your eyes <u>Close</u> listen and.

22. imagination an boy the <u>What</u> has.

23. children to music wrote poems <u>The</u> while listening.

24. showed a boy Irving <u>As</u> a great deal of charm.

25. worksheet the on sentence last the is <u>This</u>.

Theme: The William Tell Overture

Opening-
Music: Theme up and under....
Sound: Hoof-beats fade in...
Lone Ranger: Hi-yo Silver! ! !
Sound: Gunshots and hoof-beats...
Announcer: A fiery horse with the speed of light, a cloud of dust, and a
    hearty Hi-Yo Silver!  The Lone Ranger!
Music: Theme up full and under...
Announcer: With his faithful Indian companion Tonto, the daring and
    resourceful masked rider of the plains led the fight for law and order in
    the early Western United States.  Nowhere in the pages of history can
    one find a  greater champion of justice.  Return with us now to those
    thrilling days of  yesteryear....
Sound: Hoof-beats fade in...
Announcer: From out of the past come the thundering hoof-beats of the
    great horse Silver.  The Lone Ranger rides again! ! !
Lone Ranger: Come on Silver!  Let's go, big fellow!  Hi-yo Silver!  Away!
Music: Theme up full...

Ah, nostalgia!  The hoof-beats, the blazing six-shooters, the baritone
voice of the announcer, and the Willy Tell Overture all combine to make
the lead-in segment for the old Lone Ranger radio program.

Most kids are still familar with the Lone Ranger television program,
though it has faded into the sunset of non-prime time programming. How
would that very same introduction segment sound if key words were
changed? Take a look at the Master Sheet.  Certain key words have been
omitted from the text.

Prime the kids by explaining that "back before TV, weekly radio programs,
often serialized, were very popular.  One of those programs was The Lone
Ranger.  How may of you have seen the Lone Ranger on TV? (pause) Good.
Then you should be familar with the lead-in segment that begins with
each episode.

"In a moment I'm going to pass out that introduction segment, but
first...," a word from our _____.
                              *noun*

Get the kids to volunteer words that complement the ones omitted in the script. Accept words only from those who raise their hands.

Write the categories on the board and then go over each, explaining the category and accepting an example of that type of word. For instance, say: "Adjectives are words that describe, like: big, ugly, beautiful, weird, fantastic. Can someone give me a word that describes?"

Then write the suggested word on the board next to its appropriate category. After all words have been collected, hand out the Master Sheet.

Then, "Here is what we wrote as a class..." And read the introduction (dramatically), inserting the words that the kids volunteered.

Tell the kids to make up their own script, inserting words that will complete the script. I usually emphasize that they needn't worry about the label noun, adjective, etc. All they need to do is to fill-in the blank spaces so that the sentences make sense. If the sentences make sense, the inserted words will turn out to be the appropriate word type. There are some text words in parenthesises -(a) and (the). These words may or may not be used, depending upon the chosen word used in context.

After a short time, ask the kids to read their own creations aloud. Most will volunteer, or you can read several of theirs as an icebreaker.

Gear the reading to the mood of the class. If they are enjoying each other's creation, the exercise can be lengthy. If problems arise -no volunteers, obnoxious responses- end the exercise.

If the Lone Range has little relevancy or meaning for the kids that you teach, I would recommend that the same procedure be applied to *Mad Libs*. Mad Libs are compendiums of similar stories that omit appropriate word types. There are many Mad Libs publications, each in pad form. Each publication contains about twenty fill-in scripts.

*Mad Libs* are published by Price, Stern, Sloan Publishing, Inc., Los Angles, CA.

Name_____

"_____ _____."
      *exclamation*             *color*

The_____ horse with the speed of (a)_____, a
     *Adjective*                                  *noun*

cloud of dust and a hearty "Hi-yo_____," (the)_____
                              *color (above)*             *Comic -*

_____ rides again.
*book hero*

With his faithful_____ companion_____ the daring
              *noun*                       *famous person*

and resourseful_____ rider of the _____ led the
               *adjective*                  *plural noun*

fight for law and order in (the) early Western_____. Nowhere
                                    *place*

in the pages of history can one find a greater_____ of justice.
                                      *noun*

Return with us to those_____ days of yesteryear.
                    *adjective*

From out of the past comes the_____ hoofbeats of the great
                        *adjective of noise*

horse_____. The _____ rides again.
*pet animal name*     *Comic book character (above)*

" Come on_____! Let's go big fellow. Hi-yo_____! Away!
     *Color (above)*                           *Color (above)*

# Humor, or Food for Thought

Do you know they're not making wooden matches any longer?......They're long enough already! But seriously, folks, I hope that you may have been able to detect varying accents of humor throughout the foregoing sections of this menu. This section, which is indeed the savory dessert to this consuming edition, is concerned with humor as a vechicle to involve kids in education.

I recently came across an interesting article, *Did You Here the One About the Professor and the Gag Writer?* *, concerned "with a new pilot program at U.S.C. designed to make teachers more interesting to listen to, thus enhance learning." A professor 'Whose previous lectures sent whole platoons of students into the 'Land of Nod' was assisted in injecting humor into his lectures. The result of this " attempt to inject humor into pedantry....was an apparent success. As the applause indicated students liked the lecture. 'He got everything across pretty well, and it didn't drag on and on,' commented one student."

The professor spoke of the project and its main objective, saying, "You really have to convince the students that what you're teaching is exciting and relevant."

As long as educational goals are not forsaken, humor provides an excellent vehicle for learning. Humor carries with it so many positive qualities; happiness, joy, elation, aliveness, that its presence in a classroom creates an atmosphere highly receptive to a teacher's directing influence.

"Whoa, big fella," let's not get carried away! Well... Did you know there was an earthquake today?.... Yeah, and a lot of people were shaken up about it. (Come on, you can't blame me for that one, a kid told it to me! I'm innocent!)

As a Substitute Teacher, I find that my job requires me to establish my personal and teaching qualities quickly. Substitute Teachers don't experience a permanence, as do Classroom Teachers, that allows time to confront many personal, teaching, and behavorial situations present in a specific classroom. Substitutes must have an extra something to pick up the pieces where the absent teacher has left off. I find that humor helps provide that extra something. In the daily conduct of my job, I make a constant effort to use humor as frequently as the situation allows. Besides the use of humor in my lessons, I use humor in a number of other, simple ways. The following, *Humor In Kids* , presents several means I use in an attempt to capture kids in happiness, enjoyment, and learning while I am in their classroom.

*Wall Street Journal, May 17, 1974.

Teacher: "Principal, principal, the kids are revolting!"

Principal: "Well, you're pretty repulsive yourself!"

# Humor in Kids

Humor is complex. Its shades and variations draw upon an enormous repertory of language, behavior, facts, and assumptions. Adults have difficulty judging the repertory of children. They have, merely by their years, developed and filtered humor to their own satisfaction.

Kids, however, are learning about humor daily. Their sophisticated use of humor increases with age and intellectual development. In this light, humor becomes a learning process much like the experiences of language arts, mathematics, and science. And it is the teacher, realizing that humor is a learning process, who will tap the funny bones of their students at a level compatible with maturity.

It would be a shame, though, to teach humor, just as one teaches language arts, mathematics, or science. Humor is anything but a discipline. It is at once an academic aid that enriches subject matter and a psychological boost that relieves stress, buffers setbacks, and heightens enjoyment. Humor is very powerful. It has a force that captures kids and impresses a smile, a chuckle, or a warmth upon them. It quickly removes barriers that impede communication, and it instills an aliveness where dullness and inattention once prevailed.

The Classroom Teacher must recognize humor as a vehicle to involve kids in learning. The Substitute Teacher, who also must be aware of humor as a learning vehicle, can put humor to a more immediate use. Because Substitute Teachers are presented almost daily with a new situation and new kids, humor can act to relieve the awkward atmosphere associated with new classrooms, new faces, new policies, new rules, etc. I find that if I can relate to kids on a humorous level in my initial dealings with them, that is, right after the morning bell convenes class, my presence in a new classroom is less likely to become entangled in problems, confusion, and annoyances. Humor sets a mental attitude: happiness, gaiety, lightness, brightness which are so important for classroom learning.

I use varying techinques to present my humor of mental health to a new class. The *Joy At Any Price* lesson is always an enjoyable icebreaker to a morning class. Or during the morning, as I feel I am establishing a good rapport, I ask kids to tell me jokes.

I collect jokes, or so I tell the kids -this doesn't mean that you have to be a rhetorical Henny Youngman, spewing forth incessant jokes. If kids want to share their jokes before the class, I let them, though I do indicate that I am not interested in certain types of jokes.

What should you expect in the way of jokes? Ethnic jokes find contant example. For kids ethnic attachment is a presentation gimmick, they are not attuned to the many negative or degrading connotations that adults and society place on ethnic background.

Some people feel that even as a gimmick, ethnic presentations build a basis for prejudice and bigotry. You will have to resolve unto yourself how ethnic attachments should be handled.

Crude jokes tend to fall into two categories: those concerned with bodily functions and those concerned with sex. Third to sixth graders are often preoccupied with bodily functions, and seventh and eighth graders express an awareness of sex. Like ethnic attachments, you will need to establish the suitability of certain references to bodily functions and sex.

Besides many of the lessons in the Language Arts, Math, and Art sections in which I encourage humor, I also have a running presentation that I call *Pun Names* .

Pun Names are:

| | | |
|---|---|---|
| Holly Day | Sandy Eggo | Polly Wog |
| Kay Oss | Perry Chute | Aunt Eater |
| Frank Furter | Bob White | Bob Cat |
| Charlie Horse | Wind O. Payne | Annie Mole |
| Miles Anhour | Al Most | Ryan Oserous |
| Domino Boxbottom | Dan Ruff | Dianh Sauer |
| Barry Good | Terrible Typer | Barb Wire |
| Jan U. Airy | Red Wood | Mac Kreel |
| Jack Pot | C. Der Wood | Ann Chovie |
| Tubby Munchmouth | Doug Fir | Harry Ing |
| Earl Lee | Al Der | Sal Mon |
| Winny Bego | L.M. Mental | Barry Cuda |
| Des Pear | S.Q. Later | Lilly Pad |
| Chris Moss | U.R. Mean | Fern Plant |
| Ima Nutt | M.T. Glass | Mary Gold |
| Rhoda Dendron | L.E. Phant | Candy Cane |
| Chris Sandthemus | L.E. Vator | Al Mond |
| Kitty Chinn | Sally Mander | Dewey Grass |
| Otto Mobile | Ali Gator | Dirty Thistle |

I might write six pun names on the board to start the ball rolling, for instance:

|                   |                |
|-------------------|----------------|
| Tyrone Shoelaces  | Ima Nutt       |
| Barry Cuda        | Sally Mander   |
| Barb Wire         | Al Most        |

I then go down the list and explain each:

"How many of you have heard the record Basketball Jones? [An all-time Cheech and Chong classic] (pause) Good. Then you will know that Basketball Jones' real name is Tyrone Shoelaces.

"If you break Tyrone (And Tyrone is a man's name. Have you ever heard of Tyrone Powers, the movie star?) Shoelaces down, it comes out to be a phrase. Does anyone know what that phrase is ? (pause)

"That's right, 'tie-your-own-shoelaces.' (pause for giggles and snickers)

"Or there might be a woman with the first name of Ima and the last name of Nutt. That's right, 'I am a nut.' (pause, giggle, chortle)

"Who can tell me something about a truly fishy character named Barry Cuda ? (pause, response) Right, there is a barracuda fish.

"How about Sally Mander ?.:... (pause, response) Right, a salamander.

"And here is a wiry gal named Barb Wire. (pause, etc.)

"And good old Al Most. (pause) Right, the word 'almost'."

By this time they understand the pun idea and are enjoying themselves.

I usually asign a section of the blackboard for their use, to list any pun names they can think of. I tell them that if they can create their own, they can, as the day progresses, quietly come up to the board and write them down (be prepared for I.P. Freely and Harry Pits!).

Allowing the kids to list their originals doesn't detract from or interfere with the day's lessons or conduct. Of course, you must gauge the temperament of your class, but most kids won't abuse the chance to write on the board.

Sometimes I make an assignment: "By noon, I would like, from each of you, three (or more) pun names handed in on sheet of paper."

An equally enjoyable class-participation segment is an extension of Pun Names and concerns book titles. Book titles require a greater degree of sophistication and usually find great acceptance with fifth to eighth graders.

Ready for these?

> The Tragedy on the Cliff, by Eileen Dover
> Over the Cliff, by Hugo First
> Moving Stairs, by S.Q. Later
> How to Catch Butterflies, by Annette Andajar
> The Skydivers, by Perry Chute
> Up and Down, by L.E. Vator
> Monkey Kingdom, by Bab Boone
> Thunder Lizards, by Dinah Sauer
> Who Drank the Water, by M.T. Glass
> In Debt, by Owen Moore
> Postscripts, by Adeline Moore
> Traffic Perils, by Jay Walker
> The Song of the Bird, by Bob White
> The Everglades, by Ali Gator
> Jokes, by May Kimlaff
> Story of the Alphabet, by A.B. See
> Glass, by Wind O. Payne
> Early Warning, by Ray Dar
> Bagpipes, by Scott Land
> Pachyderms, by L.E. Phant
> Instruments, by Clara Nett
> Holiday on Ice, by I.C. Falls
> Creaky Door, by Russ T. Hinge
> Games People Play, by Milton Bradley

Present choice titles and authors in the same manner as the preceeding Pun Names exercise. Again you can elicit oral participation, or a written assignment.

Humor is not a magic ingredient that will solve every problem in the intricate relationships that confront kids, teachers, and administrators. But like a very choice and tempting dessert, it will quickly entice and capture most kids.